NEEV and BUDDHA

For Mom, who loves stories as much as I do.

Published by Scholastic India Pvt. Ltd.
A subsidiary of Scholastic Inc., New York, 10012 (USA).
Publishers since 1920, with international operations in Canada, Australia, New Zealand, the United Kingdom, India, and Hong Kong.

For information regarding permission, write to:
Scholastic India Pvt. Ltd.
A-27, Ground Floor, Sigma Centre
Infocity-1, Sector 34, Gurgaon-122001 (India)

First edition: June 2025

ISBN-13: 978-93-5954-474-8

Printed in India at Shivam Offset Press, New Delhi

NEEV and BUDDHA

RACHNA CHHABRIA

ILLUSTRATIONS BY
MOHIT SUNEJA

SCHOLASTIC
New York Toronto London Auckland
Sydney New Delhi Hong Kong

A NOTE FROM THE AUTHOR

I have always been fascinated with the Buddha and keen on featuring him in a book. I have also been fascinated with writing about Neev, a boy obsessed with his grades and his position as the class topper. Then, one day, the idea to merge the two entered my head. I added a scholar to this mix, and thus, Dharamjeet appeared in my story.

But how would they all meet? This question had a ready-made answer. Through a project. Now, I had to work on all the events that would happen when these three people's paths collided. That was the fun part. Finally came the crucial part. Are stories complete without friends? Definitely not.

Hope you enjoy Neev's journey and his friends as much as I did.

Neev and Buddha is a fictionalized account of a boy travelling back in time to meet the Buddha—a man he has admired and heard a lot about.

CONTENTS

1

CLASS TOPPER

Ten-year-old Neev Bhatnagar looked around the large classroom with eyes that everyone said were too large for his small face. And now, these same black eyes that he had inherited from his father were studying his classmates, scribbling away furiously to match Ms Sanika Joshi's—the history teacher—athletic pace of reading. He also had his dad's thick, black hair and his mother's slim build.

Neev's eyes widened when he saw the neat handwriting of a few students, especially that of Rishi Mathur sitting on his right and Akshay Kothari sitting on his left. These two were his arch-rivals in academics, always trying to capture his top spot in class. It was a position Neev had clung on to for three years, despite having bad handwriting.

He stared out of the window. A bird screeched, breaking his train of thought. Which bird was it? The teacher's actions snagged his attention back to the classroom. Her right hand was on the pile of report cards on her desk.

He turned towards her. Sanika Ma'am was also their class teacher. Tall and athletic, she was dressed in colourful clothes. She had a round face that now wore a grim and serious look. Her medium-length brown hair was tied in a ponytail. Her eyes, sharp as a hawk's, missed nothing that went on in class. Most pupils felt that she had two pairs of eyes—one in front and the other at the back of her head. Otherwise, how could she see what her students were up to while her back was turned towards them, to write on the blackboard?

As she lifted the bunch of report cards in her hands, a pin-drop silence fell over the class. Even the bird outside became quiet, as though it understood the seriousness of the situation. All the fifth-grade students of Shiksha Academy stared at their teacher, many mirroring her serious expression. In her floral attire, she looked like a college student instead of the strict teacher that she was.

Neev watched her intently, searching for clues. *If she stares at me before she looks at anyone else, even for a moment, then I'll know I have topped the class just like last year,* Neev thought. His mouth felt dry, and beads of sweat broke out on his forehead. The announcement of results always made him anxious. He wiped his hands on the sides of his shorts. All of a sudden, he felt stuffy. He loosened the collar of his shirt as though it was choking him.

From the corner of his eyes, he saw Rishi watching him. Studious looking and skinny to the point of being all bones, he sat stiffly in his seat. Rishi's square face was always grim, like it had forgotten to smile. A pointed nose and a sharp chin made his face stand out during class photographs at his previous school. Most people complimented him on his thick, black hair, which needed several combings before he could leave for school. This bird's nest that he carried on his head was both his best and worst feature. It depended on its mood.

Ever since Rishi joined Shiksha Academy a year ago, he had impressed the teachers with his homework, well-researched assignments, extra neat handwriting, and his wonderful behaviour. His good grades had made Neev nervous and jittery. If he wasn't careful, this perfect student would soon overtake him and push him to the second spot.

Sanika Ma'am's eyes rested on Neev's face for the briefest of seconds, then they focused on Rishi. Neev's heart soared like a bird in the sky. Yay! He was the class topper this year, too. Fiercely possessive about his grades and his position, he guarded his homework and assignments like it was a top-secret, Code Red mission.

Adjusting the stack of report cards, Sanika Ma'am stared at the students. 'As usual, there were some students who made me proud, and a few who should definitely put in more effort,' she said.

Several students gulped, and a few trembled, perhaps anticipating the reaction from their parents.

'With a total of 971, Neev Bhatnagar takes the top spot,' she called out the first name.

The class broke into applause. Even the ones shaking like jelly put all their energy into the act of clapping, more to steady their tremors.

As Sanika Ma'am walked towards his desk, Neev's heart started doing bhangra inside his body.

'Very good, Neev. Keep up the good work,' she said and handed the report card to the silent boy. 'Improve your handwriting. I have deducted marks for the untidy writing.'

Neev gasped. He blinked back the tears pooling around his eyes. Accepting the report card from the teacher, he took a moment to look at his marks. With an A+ grade in all subjects and marks above ninety, he had plenty of reasons to be happy. But sadly, his eyes were focused on the five marks the teacher had deducted from his total.

'Rishi Mathur,' Sanika Ma'am called the second name. 'The difference between your total and Neev's total is just one mark,' she smiled. 'I'm sure next time you two will be equal.'

Rishi was quiet. Tears spilled out from his eyes. He had tried so hard, but that one mark had eluded him.

Neev wiped the moisture from his own eyes. These five marks had turned out to be traitors, like friends who snuck to the teacher behind one's back. If not for them, he would have beaten Rishi by six marks.

'Buck up, Neev,' Veda Verma whispered into his ear from the seat behind. Her large eyes watched him. A grin was plastered on her oval face. Two plaits tamed her shoulder-length wavy brown hair. Her shirt and shorts were spotlessly clean and creaseless. Her black shoes and her white socks were worthy of being photographed. Every student wondered how she managed to keep them so clean throughout the day.

Veda's daredevil attitude frightened everyone in class. 'If you aren't careful, Rishi will soon overtake you. Poof, and your top spot will disappear,' she grinned. Though she never topped the class, she was a good student and content with her ranking in the top five. The only complaint teachers had about Veda was her bad habit of constantly chewing gum in class. Whenever a teacher asked her a question, the gum would almost always find its way to the underside of her desk.

There were rumours that she had exchanged her desk with others in the classroom—no wonder most tables had gum stuck underneath them. Veda was also the class monitor, a fact that silenced most students. No one wanted her to dock marks from their houses for being rude to a prefect. This was also the sole reason why the students did not touch the bottom of their desks. If that happened by accident, they would immediately sanitize their hands.

Turning to Rishi, Veda said, 'Who cries for one mark? Stop acting like a baby!'

Ignoring her comment, Rishi sat down in his chair. 'Congratulations,' he whispered to Neev.

Neev nodded. Though he wanted to console Rishi, he refrained from doing so. Ever since Rishi had joined Shiksha Academy, he had tried being friends with Neev and often requested if he could sit with him while doing assignments in the library. Neev had rebuffed all the offers. He was scared Rishi would copy his homework and assignments.

Akshay, who was sitting close to Neev, turned towards him. The tall boy with curly hair had an odd look on his face. Several expressions flickered in his chocolate brown eyes. The final one left Neev quite confused. Was Akshay frowning or scowling? Was there a question in his eyes or a dark look? A perplexed Neev averted his gaze.

Neev had turned down his offers of friendship, too. Though they had been classmates from first grade, they were not friends. If Akshay focused more on academics and less on cricket, especially watching replays of Virat Kohli's batting, he would be the numero uno in class. He was the best batsman of the school, and students thronged the grounds to watch him play. His sixes and fours were a joy to watch, evoking a frenzy from his teammates and the students of his house.

There were rumours that he would become the captain of Shiksha Academy's Junior School Cricket Team in the next few weeks. Akshay was friends with everyone in class, though he hung out mostly with Sunny and Minku, the brown-haired, brown-eyed, slim twins. They were die-hard football fans and played for the school's football team. Most people were always confused between the two brothers because more often than not, they even had the same expression on their faces.

Sadly, Neev had no friends in school. Shy and withdrawn, he was always quiet and also very, very suspicious. He always doubted his classmates' motives. As the other students put their report cards in their bags, with their expressions ranging from relief to horror, Neev pulled out a notebook from his bag to practise his handwriting.

'Oh no,' he muttered. He had mistakenly brought his mother's notebook. Her name, Neha Bhatnagar, was written on the top. His mother was a Buddhist scholar and a professor at Bhopal's Sanchi University of Buddhist–Indic Studies. Books on the Buddha and Buddhism filled their bookshelves at home. Last night, both his mom and he were working at the dining table. Their notebooks looked alike, and he must have accidentally tucked hers into his school bag as well.

I hope Mom doesn't need this notebook at the university today, he thought, staring at it in dismay. *Else I'm in deep trouble.*

Neev moved his mother's notebook aside and then brought out his own. As his writing filled the page, Neev pulled a face. How could his words resemble two extra hairy and angry millipedes fighting each other on a white page?

The teacher cleared her throat. 'Now, I have an announcement to make. It's not because I'm being partial. But with this new system, I hope to motivate and inspire you all to do better next time. This year, the class topper will choose the topic for the annual project. Neev, go ahead,' she looked at him.

Neev gulped. This was a surprise. His eyes fell on his mother's notebook. Out of all the blurred words, only a single word stood out.

'Buddha,' he said quickly.

From his childhood, Neev had been a huge admirer of the Buddha. He stared with fascination at the Buddha statues and paintings adorning his house and watched his mother practise her Buddhist meditation.

'Now comes the surprise,' Sanika Ma'am said. Her eyes twinkled as she focused on Neev. 'This project will require teamwork. Each team will have four students. I aim to teach everyone about working to one's strengths and building trust in your teammates. So, I will be deciding the members this time. Neev, your team will be Veda, Akshay, and Rishi.'

2

IT'S NARU

Before Neev could lift his jaw from the floor where it had crashed after Sanika Ma'am's announcement, she dropped another bomb.

'Each team will have two months to complete their project. The best one in the class will be our entry in the Inter-school Assignment Competition. The best projects from each school get a direct entry into this competition. The first prize is ₹50,000, shared equally among the members of the winning team.'

All the students, even those upset about their report cards, were excited at the mention of the prize money.

The class broke into an excited chatter, not paying attention to the fact that the teacher was still in the room. Sanika Ma'am continued calling out the names of the students of the other teams. Some were happy; a few made faces at the teammates they were stuck with. Sunny and Minku frowned because they were put in different groups. Siya had tears in her eyes as she was separated from Veda, her best friend. They sat next to each other, and both looked so alike that they could be mistaken for sisters. The same height, the similar faces. They even wore their wavy hair in matching hairstyles. The difference was that Siya was quiet, while Veda was an explosion of noise.

'It's OK, don't cry,' Veda patted her best friend's hand. Siya nodded tearfully. Both the girls wanted to be scientists and constantly hung around the science laboratory in their free time.

As soon as Sanika Ma'am left the classroom, the students huddled with their teammates and started making plans. Within seconds, Neev was pulled towards Veda's desk by his team members.

'Let's give our dream team a name,' Veda said. 'I suggest NARV. For Neev, Akshay, Rishi, and Veda. It's nerve pronounced with an *a* and minus the last *e*. I hope you all like it. If you don't, come up with a better suggestion,' she said confidently, as though she was challenging them.

'Super, I like it,' Akshay thumped the table, making the eraser jump in the air like a startled grasshopper.

'Me too,' Rishi added.

Neev nodded. NARV did sound nice. Veda was a quick thinker.

'So that's sorted,' she said. 'I'll be the spokesperson of the team, the public face, as I'm the friendliest out of you all.' Veda smiled, convinced she was doing them all a big favour.

Rishi said, 'I will be the second in command, the research analyst. Neev will be the main researcher.'

'What about me?' Akshay demanded.

'With your sports background, you'll do all the running around to find good quality chart paper, sketch pens, colour pens, glue, and photos that will enhance our project. Mind you, we all will pool in the money, but you will be our project coordinator, the assignment organizer,' Veda explained.

Akshay looked pleased with his job profile. The project coordinator sounded like it encompassed many important responsibilities.

'Every weekend, we will gather in one house and work on the project. We are lucky that we all live nearby, so it won't be any trouble meeting up,' Veda, the self-appointed spokesperson, said.

Neev rolled his eyes. This dream team was going to be a nightmare for him. He was already getting a headache with all the plans Veda was throwing around.

'Let's all play to our strengths,' she said.

'All of you will be handing over your library cards to Neev, and he will choose the books to research from,' Akshay announced. 'His assignments always get the highest marks.

So, let's tap into his talent of choosing the best books.'

'But I will do the actual writing of the project,' Rishi said. 'We can't afford to lose marks because of Neev's bad handwriting.'

Neev's handwriting was indeed becoming a nuisance and always cropping up in conversations, both at home and in school.

'From today onwards, all of you will be reading as much as you can about the Buddha,' Veda ordered. 'Jot down all the important points neatly, so we can read what you have written.' She then looked at Neev pointedly and added, '...and share your research with others.'

The boys nodded.

'And no discussing the project with anyone else, not even your best friends,' she warned, 'I have eyes and ears all over the school. Even the faintest whiff of a rumour will get to me.'

'If anyone finds any links online, then please share them with the others. Send it to everyone's email IDs, as we won't be using the school email,' Rishi said. 'That will ensure that there are no leaks from our side.'

These people are beating me at being suspicious, Neev thought.

'Though with Neev in our team, there is nothing to worry about. The top spot will be ours. But as they say, "don't count your chickens before they hatch",' Veda grinned.

'Everyone will be always on alert,' Rishi added.

Neev's head was spinning like a top. He clutched the desk for support. By the time he realized that it was a 'chewing gum' table, he had accidentally touched a lump of gum stuck to the bottom. *Oh no,* he groaned, dropping his hands by his sides. He needed to sanitize his hands as soon as possible or at least wash them.

If Veda, Rishi, and Akshay went on like the way they were going on now, he was in for a rough time. So far, he had aced all his assignments and projects because he had always been a lone ranger. Teamwork was something else. It was definitely not his forte. Would he be able to maintain his winning streak? Share resources? Be a team player and take orders from his teammates? Especially the bossy Veda?

Neev's mouth felt dry. Sitting down on Veda's chair, he stared at his team. They watched him warily, as though he was going to attack them.

Think Neev think, he muttered. *Get out of this situation.*

An idea popped into his mind.

'I need to go to the toilet,' he told the others.

They nodded, continuing their whispered discussion.

Neev rushed out of the classroom. The first stop he made was to the restroom to wash his hands with soap. Then he raced down the corridor to the staffroom. It was a spacious and airy room painted a pale yellow. The windows were flung open, letting in a good amount of sunshine and a cool breeze.

It had comfortable chairs, single-seater sofas, and a large table in its centre. Many of the teachers had returned to their seats. Sanika Ma'am sat on a sofa, sipping a cup of tea and munching cookies.

Neev looked pleased. Tea and cookies always made people feel good. So, this was the perfect time to pitch his request.

As he made his way towards her, the teacher looked up.

'Yes, Neev?' she raised her eyebrows.

'Can I do the project all by myself?' he asked nervously.

'Why?'

'I'm not too sure I'll be able to work with other students,' he replied. 'And their assignments never get high marks as they never do good research.'

'Then isn't it all the more better that you all work in teams?' she said.

Neev fell silent. He cursed his brain, it just wasn't helping him by refusing to think of a single workable excuse.

'If I remember correctly, you hope to become a neurosurgeon in the future?' she asked.

Neev nodded.

'Can you perform a surgery alone, without anyone assisting you?' she asked, looking into his eyes.

Neev lowered his head. He wished he hadn't announced to the class what his ambition was. Now, Sanika Ma'am was holding that against him. Just like parents, teachers could twist your words to your disadvantage.

'This project is about team effort and embracing each other's strengths and weaknesses,' she said. 'If you refuse to be a team player and insist on going solo, I'll be deducting twenty-five marks from your final total.'

Neev gasped. Twenty-five marks would push him close to the twentieth rank in class. Then, he could wave goodbye to his top spot.

3

BUDDHA, HELP ME PLEASE

All through the bus journey home, Neev was quiet. Veda had insisted that NARV sit together as a part of a team bonding exercise. She had dragged him from his seat at the front to the last row, which she usually occupied. Luckily, neither Siya nor Sunny and Minku were in the same school bus as they stayed in different neighbourhoods.

He looked out from the window. The traffic in Bhopal at this time was sparse. A few cars whizzed past them, and so did several scooterists. People holding umbrellas to protect themselves from the sun waited at the signal to cross the road.

'Why are they out of their houses at this time of the afternoon?' Neev muttered.

The bus cruised at a steady pace, passing familiar sights.

'I'll be emailing regular updates to all of you,' Veda whispered.

His eyes on the road, ears listening to his team's conversation, Neev was a mute spectator who was content to listen to their plans.

'I check my emails twice a day as I write to all my favourite cricketers,' Akshay announced.

'Do they reply?' Veda asked curiously.

'Some do,' he said proudly.

'Please don't expect me to reply immediately,' Rishi pleaded. 'My mom gets angry if I use my laptop when I'm studying or doing homework.'

Veda nodded.

Neev continued staring out of the window, his mind a jumble of thoughts. How was he to get out of this situation? Would Sanika Ma'am agree to his request of going solo if he went to the principal? Would any excuse work on them? How was he to explain to them that he had better chances of winning if he worked alone and at his pace?

The bus veered towards the lane leading to his house. Neev stood up and started walking towards the door.

'Bye,' he said curtly.

'See ya tomorrow,' Veda said cheerfully.

'Bye, dude,' Akshay thumped his back.

'Bye Neev,' Rishi piped in.

Neev's brow furrowed with concern. His teammates were getting quite friendly with him. The boundaries he had drawn around himself hadn't stopped them at all. They had all climbed over it the moment Sanika Ma'am had announced their names as one team.

Jumping down from the bus, Neev walked quickly towards his house. Pushing open the gate, he strode towards the main door. Neera, their domestic help, opened it even before he rang the doorbell. She always kept an eye out for his bus. She was a fashion-crazy girl, always falling victim to the latest trends. This time, it was a parachute skirt that swept a 12-inch area around her. No wonder the house was spick and span, as her skirt constantly glided all over the house.

'Your mom has baked a cake for you. Do you want a slice?' she asked.

'No,' Neev replied. 'Where is Mom?'

'Meditating in her room.'

That meant she didn't want to be disturbed, Neev thought. She must be more stressed than she is showing. Whenever his mother was over-stressed, she baked cakes and cookies.

Ditching his school bag in his bedroom, he grabbed the fruit and milk from the tray Neera had placed on his study table.

He had half-an-hour of internet before his house's Wi-Fi went into lockdown mode. His parents were strict about his screen time.

He opened the laptop he shared with his mom. The Buddha stared at him from the screen. Serene and blissful. This was his mother's favourite screensaver.

Neev quickly typed in 'Excuses To Get Out Of A Situation'. The search engine threw up hundreds of ideas: getting kidnapped by aliens, being trapped inside a lion's cage in the zoo, swallowed by giant rats, and ghosts barricading his door. The best excuse by far was that his parents had shifted to Mars.

'Hmm, none of these will work on Sanika Ma'am. She is way too smart to fall for these pathetic excuses,' he muttered.

Ping.

A notification popped up on his laptop.

It was an email from Veda.

'Welcome to NARV. The dream team consisting of the fabulous four.' It was accompanied by a collage of all their pictures.

Neev's eyes widened. There was no respite from his teammates. They were stalking him everywhere like overfriendly ghosts. Then, a thought crossed his mind. Where had she got their pictures from?

Before he could think of a reply, he saw Akshay's answer: 'Proud to be a NARVian.'

Neev started typing a message, then he deleted it. He definitely wasn't excited to be a part of NARV. He toyed with the idea of ignoring Veda's email. Then he decided against it. He would be polite.

'Same here,' Neev typed and hit the Send button.

It would be some time before Rishi would see all the messages.

Shutting his laptop a good twenty minutes before his scheduled time was up, Neev changed out of his school uniform into a faded T-shirt and shorts and went to his garden.

Red and white roses welcomed him, suffusing the air with their scent. The garden was his mother's passion and a labour of her hard work. She spent a lot of time with her plant babies, singing to them, watering them, and taking care of them.

Like Buddha, Neev decided to meditate under a tree and look for solutions to get out of NARV and make it just Team N.

Closing his eyes, he sat cross-legged under the mango tree, trying to focus on his breath like his mother did every morning as soon as she woke up. A crow cawed from high up in the branches, attracting a bunch of noisy crows. A couple of mosquitoes decided to quench their thirst by sucking his blood.

I should have applied mosquito repellent. Neev opened one eye and swatted away the large mosquito.

Once again, he closed his eyes. There was silence for some time as the insects left him alone. 'Perhaps my blood isn't tasty as I thought,' he muttered. A helicopter flew past. Its familiar

noise was music to his ears. Neev loved choppers. Though tempted to open his eyes, Neev refrained from doing so. 'No distractions,' he chanted.

A fruit fell on his head and rolled down into his lap.

Neev frowned. Was this his 'aha' moment? Like Isaac Newton, would he, too, suddenly come up with an answer for his problem? But going by the size of the fruit, it was more of an 'ouch' moment.

Neev reluctantly opened his eyes and rubbed his head. He tried to feel for a bump. The area felt sore. 'Hope I don't get a lump tomorrow,' he muttered.

A small monkey jumped down from the tree. The animal eyed the huge mango in his lap. Neev's eyes widened. It was a giant mango. Before he could react, the monkey quickly grabbed the mango and darted up the tree.

Neev wondered how Buddha had meditated for so many days. He could barely focus for a minute without something distracting him.

He closed his eyes once again. For a few seconds, there was silence. *The crow was finally quiet*, he thought with relief.

His relief, though, was short-lived. A warm liquid slid down his arm.

'Oh no,' he groaned, opening his eyes again. The reason for the crow's silence became apparent. It was in poop mode.

He stared at the left sleeve of his T-shirt. It looked as

though not one crow, but the entire lot had together pooped on him. Rushing into his house, he changed his clothes. He once again returned to his meditating place. Sitting cross-legged under the tree, he was determined to get some answers this time.

A gentle breeze rustled his clothes, whispering against his skin and hair. A worm crawled over his knee.

Neev felt a warm wetness on his hand once again. He reluctantly opened his eyes. Goosebumps erupted on his arms as he stared at the doe, licking his hand.

Where had it come from? He had never seen a baby deer in his neighbourhood or even in his city. The few that existed remained inside the confines of a zoo, not interested in licking the hands of a meditating ten-year-old boy.

He looked around, blinking in surprise. His house had disappeared. He looked up. The mango tree, too, had disappeared. There was a different strange tree looking down at him. A shiver ran down his spine.

A presence made him look to his side.

Buddha sat opposite to him. He was wearing his orange robes, and his hair was coiled in a bun on top of his head. He watched Neev with a gentle smile on his peaceful face.

'So, Neev, you wanted to meet me? Buddha said.

4

MEETING THE BUDDHA

'How can I improve my handwriting?' Neev blurted out. 'Once my handwriting gets better, my class teacher and other teachers won't deduct marks from my total.'

'Neev, you have to make a conscious effort to improve your handwriting. Daily practise will take you far,' Buddha replied. 'With time, effort, and lots of patience, your handwriting will improve.'

'Isn't there a shortcut?' Neev asked.

'No,' was Buddha's single-word reply. 'Shortcuts don't always work in life. To reach your goals, you will always have to go on a journey.'

'Okay. Now, please tell me how can I get out of NARV?' he asked. Then he explained to Buddha about what happened at school and how NARV was formed. 'I don't want to do any project with Akshay, Rishi, and Veda.'

'Why?' Again a single word, but this time posed as a question.

'Why should I share my marks with them?' Neev asked. 'I'm sure if I did the project alone, mine will be the best.'

'Confidence is a good attribute, but overconfidence isn't good. Don't underestimate your friends. Each one will bring their strength to the project. You can't do everything alone, but together you all can do something.'

'But I've to share all my research with them.' Neev looked sad.

'So?'

Neev fell silent. He watched the birds on the tree. The doe had moved away from him and was now grazing grass a little distance away. Perhaps it had not liked the taste of Neev's hand. Bored of eating the grass, the young animal approached them and sat down beside Buddha. It stared at the sage with adoring eyes.

'Please tell me how to get out of NARV,' Neev pleaded again, this time with tears in his eyes.

Buddha stared at him with a penetrating gaze. It was a look that laid bare his heart and all his feelings.

'Some journeys are meant to be taken in a group,' Buddha replied. 'What are you trying to hide, Neev? It's time you made friends. It's time you trusted people.'

Neev was silent.

'I don't understand how Rishi, Veda, and Akshay can help me,' he said quietly.

'They will share their research with you,' Buddha continued. 'Who knows? Their research may be better than yours, Neev.'

Neev looked surprised. No one could do research better than him.

A few sparrows swooped down beside them, pecking the grass as though they were searching for seeds.

'Your handwriting may continue to cost you extra marks,' Buddha said with a faraway look on his face. 'Don't you feel you have to stop being so possessive and obsessive about your marks?'

'But the first spot has been mine for three years.'

'The best thing about any spot in life is that it can change anytime. Whenever one of your classmates works hard, they can overtake you and claim that spot,' Buddha said. 'You, too, claimed it from someone.'

'Yes, I overtook Karun, who was a topper.' Neev was surprised that Buddha knew that the first spot hadn't always been his.

'Imagine how Karun must have felt when he saw you in his place?'

'But I worked hard to claim it,' Neev explained.

'By that logic, anyone who works hard can claim the prize, right?' Buddha asked.

Neev lowered his gaze.

'If Karun was still in your school, you would have had to face tough competition for that first place,' Buddha said.

Neev nodded. Karun's father had been transferred to Chennai. So, the entire family had shifted there at the end of second grade. Neev had been in the second spot in that year, several marks behind Karun. But with him leaving school, he had become the class topper. Since then, he had fiercely protected the spot.

'This joint project will be a blessing for you. Trust me, it will work to your advantage. It will give you the time to improve your handwriting, which will serve you well in the long run. You will gain friends. Good friends you can trust. Friends who will have your back. Friends who will come to your rescue when you need it the most,' Buddha said.

Neev's eyes widened.

'Will I be getting into trouble or into a situation where I need to be rescued?' he asked.

Buddha smiled. A smile that neither confirmed nor denied Neev's question. 'Let some things in life remain a mystery.'

Neev badly wanted to ask the question that had been weighing him down. He was desperate to share the secret he had been carrying in his heart for a long time with Buddha. The question always filled him with sadness. But as usual, Neev's hesitation didn't allow him to be open, even with the Buddha.

'Any more questions, Neev?'

'You are leaving so fast?' he asked, reluctant to let Buddha leave.

'We will meet again soon. Perhaps by then you will trust me enough to share all your secrets,' Buddha replied. Once again, the mysterious smile appeared on his face. 'Think about what we discussed, and make the right decision.'

Gently patting Neev's head, Buddha faded away into the air. The doe disappeared. So did the tree they were sitting under.

'What just happened?' Neev was puzzled. He looked around his garden. He was back under the mango tree. The crows had started cawing as though they were arguing.

He mulled over Buddha's words. If he wanted to retain his top spot, he was stuck with Rishi, Akshay, and Veda. Nothing in this world could get him out of NARV now.

This was one situation the class topper couldn't escape, no matter what he did.

5

PICNIC IN THE GARDEN

It was quite some time since Neev had returned from visiting the Buddha. Though physically he was sitting stiffly under the mango tree and trying to gather his scattered thoughts, his mind kept replaying the innumerable fights he had seen at home between his parents. It had resulted in their separation.

The young boy was feeling bad that he hadn't told Buddha about the biggest problem troubling him: his parents' divorce. He was unable to shake off his gloom. This sorrow weighed heavily on his shoulders as though all the burdens of the world sat there.

He wondered what had gone wrong in his parents' lives. In his perfect life, he used to call his parents and himself the 'Terrific Trio'. They would do so many things together. Play carrom, go for jogs, watch movies, and even do gardening as a team. Now, he had just his mother for company, and her unhappiness matched his.

Neev badly wished he could talk to someone. It would have been wonderful to have a sibling. Even a chatterbox like Veda, a crazy sports fan like Akshay, or a serious boy like Rishi would have sufficed. Anything would have been better than being alone.

Sadly, he wasn't close to any of his cousins. He had always turned down their efforts to get to know each other, just like he had done in school for all his classmates (especially Akshay and Rishi). A sibling or a cousin would have been a blessing.

Their words would have comforted him. Their presence would have been a welcome change from the solitude surrounding him. But for an introvert like him, revealing his family's problems to friends wasn't easy.

And then there was always the issue of trust. Neev was scared that if he confided in a classmate, they would reveal his secrets to the entire class. That would make him the butt of all their jokes. Brushing his tears away, Neev turned his attention to his house.

Suddenly, he saw his mom approaching him from the verandah, her eyes red, like she, too, had been crying. As she sat down next to him, Neev noticed that she was looking frail and there were dark circles under her eyes. Her long face had the saddest look he had ever seen, as though someone had pulled down the corners of her lips.

Averting his gaze from his mother, he studied the Buddha statue in the garden. The figure was seated in the lotus posture. Its eyes were closed. They had bought the statue on their last holiday to Bhutan. Neev had chosen it from the vast collection the shop had housed. It was his favourite image of Buddha. Every time he walked past it, he paused for a few seconds to study the serene expression on the wise sage's face.

'Mom, I chose the Buddha as the topic of our class project in school today,' he suddenly said.

'That's wonderful,' she replied. 'If you want to read my

notes for extra research, I'll happily lend them to you.'

'But I've got to share them with my teammates,' he made a disgruntled face. 'Sanika Ma'am has put us in teams. My teammates are Akshay, Rishi, and Veda.'

'What a lovely idea,' she smiled, and it lit up her face.

'I don't want to be a part of any team,' Neev sulked.

'It's high time you made friends. Teamwork will teach you many things. And what is this nonsense about not sharing your notes with your teammates?' she said sternly. 'You must change this attitude. This project will work to your advantage, and you will gain friends.'

Neev was quiet. His mother was talking just like Buddha. For a moment he thought of confiding about his meeting with Buddha to his mom. Would she believe him? Or dismiss it as a figment of his imagination?

The silence was broken by a loud chatter, shattering Neev's train of thought. He turned to the main gate of his house. His eyes widened in both shock and surprise.

His teammates were walking through the main gate as though it was something they did daily.

'Hello, Aunty,' Veda said. She carried a basket in one hand.

Akshay and Rishi also greeted his mom.

'Hello, kids,' she greeted them warmly. She had met them a few times during the parent–teacher meetings in school. 'It's lovely to see you all. I'll send some cake for everybody.'

His mother stood up. Brushing off the leaves and dust from her trousers, she started walking towards the house.

'What are you doing sitting under the tree?' Akshay asked.

'Don't tell me that you are meditating?' Rishi said, plonking down beside him.

Veda watched him with serious eyes.

'Were you crying?' she asked.

She was the only one who had spotted the dampness around his eyes. She was observant and sharp.

'If you want to discuss anything with me, you can,' she said. 'All my friends confide in me, and their secrets are always safe with me.'

'Your secret will be safe with me, too,' Rishi said.

'Me three,' Akshay nodded.

The trio watched him intently for several moments. Neev was silent. He felt he was being studied by his teammates.

'Dude, this was *so* not my idea,' Akshay said finally, breaking the silence.

'I wasn't in favour of it, too,' Rishi agreed.

What were they saying? Neev wondered. A flicker of hope flared in his heart. *Were Veda, Rishi, and Akshay talking of not being part of this joint project?*

Alas, that wasn't the case.

'We are talking about this sudden visit to your house. It

was Veda's idea. She wanted our team to spend time together and to get to know each other well before we started working,' Rishi said.

Veda deposited the picnic hamper beside him. When she removed the cover, he saw sandwiches, muffins, and juice.

Neera entered the garden carrying a tray loaded with chocolate cake, cookies, and paper napkins. Placing it before the children, she returned to the house.

Neev was dismayed. No Team N. There was no escaping these three. If someone had told him that he would be having a picnic with a few of his classmates in his garden, he would have scoffed at them. He would have dismissed their words as a bad joke. The three people he had spent the entire year avoiding were now comfortably sitting in his garden, munching on snacks.

'Your mom makes the best cake in the world,' Rishi said.

'I'll ask my mother to ask yours for the recipe,' Akshay sighed. 'I can eat this every day.'

'Athletes have to be careful about their diet,' Veda said. 'So, you can't have cake every day,' she grinned.

'Thank you, Ms Know-it-all,' Akshay made a face.

Listening to their chatter, Neev reluctantly admitted to himself that their presence had diverted his mind from his problems.

Leaning close to him, Veda whispered in his ears. 'I thought you could do with some cheering up today.'

Like Neev, she was an only child. Their mothers were college friends and had tried to forge a bond between their children. But they had failed every time because of Neev's reluctance to make friends.

Neev looked at her. Her eyes were kind and understanding and made him blink back his tears. She knew about his secret. Would she sneak to his classmates?

6

BUDDHA EVERYWHERE

On Friday, the NARV members met at Neev's house (again). Much to his dismay, his house had become NARV's official meeting place. To beat the heat, they were all wearing light cotton shorts and T-shirts. Bhopal was experiencing a scorching summer. Despite it being late evening, beads of sweat ran down their faces as they entered the cool confines of his living room, their hair was coated with perspiration.

Akshay sat on the single-seater sofa, directly underneath the fan, earning disapproving looks from Rishi and Veda.

'It's nice to see you all bonding,' Neev's mom emerged from the kitchen with a tray in her hands.

The children's eyes brightened when they saw the tall glasses of cold lemonade, mint leaves floating on top. Alongside was a plateful of large chocolate chip cookies. Sipping on lemony drinks and munching on cookies made them forget the heat instantly.

'These are too good,' Rishi said, helping himself to his second cookie. His friends were on their third one.

'I've tickets for an exhibition of Buddhist paintings,' Veda announced excitedly, as if it were tickets to the final football match between Spain and Argentina. 'Luckily, the venue is an art gallery close to all our homes.'

The boys stared open-mouthed at her. Bossy Veda was surely making a lot of plans for them.

'To create the best project, we need to think out of the box,' she said.

'And going to an exhibition will help us nail the project?' Rishi asked. 'There is so much we can do. I think this outing will unnecessarily waste our precious time and energy. And it's so hot.'

'What exactly were you planning to do?' Veda asked, her hands on her waist. 'Read more books. Come on, boys! Think beyond books.'

Neev wasn't very pleased with Veda's plans.

'You two always have your noses buried inside books. The other day, I saw a silverfish on both your noses,' she said with a serious expression on her face.

Rishi exchanged an alarmed look with Neev.

'Boys, she's joking,' Akshay laughed.

'These two thought I was serious,' Veda grinned. 'It's so easy to fool them.'

Neev and Rishi shook their heads. Madam V would drive them mad.

'We will go separately to the venue tomorrow. Take a longer route to mislead any classmates spying on us,' she instructed them. 'A lot of them live in the same area as us.'

The boys stared at her.

'Don't roll your eyes at me, Neev,' Veda said, turning to him. 'I've learnt this secrecy from you.'

On Saturday morning, Neev walked to the art gallery to meet his teammates. He decided to leave a little before the scheduled time and keep a lookout for classmates lurking at the back of the trees or hiding behind cars.

Sadly, Neev bumped into someone the second he stepped outside. It was Mihir Mehta, a classmate.

'Hey, Neev! Where are you going?' Mihir asked excitedly as he stopped his cycle next to Neev.

'Going for a walk,' he replied.

'It's good to exercise,' Mihir smiled. 'I didn't know that you were into fitness.'

'What are you doing outside my house?' Neev asked.

'I'm visiting my aunt who lives nearby,' Mihir said too quickly, turning his face away.

He is lying, Neev thought. *Veda was right. His classmates were keeping an eye on him and watching his moves.*

Mihir cycled slowly so that he matched Neev's pace. Neev walked past the art gallery without even looking at it, pretending to be unaware of its existence.

As they moved past the building, Mihir said goodbye and, making a U-turn, cycled away and veered into a lane on the right.

Neev quickly turned around and ran back to the small bungalow housing the art gallery. Luckily for him, the gate was easy to open. He looked back; there was no sign of Mihir.

His friends were huddled behind a tree near the entrance.

'What took you so long?' Veda asked.

'Mihir was spying on me,' Neev blurted out.

'I told you,' Veda said. 'Human psychology is not your strong point. You boys are hopeless. If it wasn't for me, everyone would be aware of all your plans.'

For once, the boys secretly agreed with Veda.

The bungalow, freshly painted in a warm blue, had a pleasant and welcoming look. Red, pink, and purple bougainvillea flowers bloomed on the vines. In one corner of the garden was a jasmine tree. The air was filled with the scent of its flowers.

'This is so pretty,' Veda sighed, clicking a few pictures with her mobile phone.

Climbing up the steps, the team walked into the bungalow. The owners had converted it into a gallery for exhibitions, renting it out to different creators to showcase their talents.

They entered the hall where the Buddhist paintings were being displayed. There was complete silence. Four people ahead of them studied the paintings. The first painting was of Buddha's mother, Queen Mahamaya, sleeping peacefully. A full moon was visible outside her window, casting a silver halo and bathing the surroundings in a special glow. Attendants guarded her room. The queen dreamt that a white elephant entered her body.

'This painting looks so beautiful,' Neev said, reading the words beneath. He opened his notebook to copy the accompanying information.

'Don't,' Veda held his hand. Taking out her phone, she clicked several pictures of the painting and the writing on the placard beside it. 'Mom has allowed me to borrow her spare phone,' she explained.

They stood before the painting for several minutes, studying the soft colours that the artist, Anamika Das, had used.

The next painting was again of Queen Mahamaya. But this time, she was in the Lumbini Grove. She was under a sal tree, her hand on the trunk, giving birth to a child. The foliage on the trees was a dark green, making it seem as if the entire grove was in an excited mood.

In the next painting, the baby boy took seven steps, and lotuses bloomed at every step.

Rishi read the words beneath the artwork. 'The lotuses symbolize the purity and sanctity of the baby's arrival into the world.' Then, he added, 'This is just so beautiful. See how the different stages of Buddha's life are depicted in these paintings.'

Neev was enchanted with the art. Each portrait told a story in itself. A young Buddha playing in the palace. The Buddha when he was a small boy, studying with the rishis.

Neev stood beside a painting of a young Buddha sitting in a chariot. This painting showed a turning point in the Buddha's life. It had the four signs in succession: an old man, a sick person, a corpse being carried to its cremation, and a monk meditating beneath a tree.

Neev then studied the painting of Buddha meditating under the bodhi tree. It reminded him of their meeting and the short conversation they had had a few days ago. The next painting was of Buddha in the Deer Park, delivering his first sermon to his followers.

'Even if this trip doesn't throw up any exciting ideas in our heads about the project, it has been worth it just for the brilliance of these paintings,' Rishi said.

Though Neev agreed with his teammate, he didn't voice his thoughts.

Neev noticed Veda staring at him—like Buddha had done. It was a profound look, one that peeped into his heart and discovered all the secrets he had tucked comfortably inside.

Neev realized that Veda had known today was the day of his parents' divorce. Neev's mother must have told Veda's mother; they often chatted on the phone for a long time.

He turned his face away and pretended to look at another painting. His friends strolled ahead. Neev realized that Veda had deliberately organized this outing to distract him. His perspective towards Veda changed. Inside that non-stop chatterbox was a sensitive and kind person. A perfect friend anyone would like to have.

7

IDEAS, AND MORE IDEAS

Neev's mind had turned into a large cauldron bubbling with ideas. He looked around, absorbing the paintings like a sponge. Everything in the exhibition was inspirational, giving him several thoughts on how to tackle their project. The large leaves of the sal trees, the light pink hue of the lotuses, the pristine beauty of the white elephant, the expressions on the faces of the herd of deer, and even the palace where Buddha lived—each element ignited possibilities. Ideas were swirling in Neev's mind like low-lying mist. This had never happened to him before. His body throbbed with excitement.

He watched his teammates. They looked normal, which meant they weren't experiencing what Neev was so clearly undergoing. Rishi was chewing his lower lip as he looked at a painting. Akshay had been staring at another one for several minutes, perhaps hoping to pick up a trick or two to improve his craft (his sketching skills were the best in class). Veda was clicking pictures of the information written on the placards.

Neev looked around. Beside them, there were only a few others in the art gallery. So, it was perfectly safe to discuss their plans.

'I have a few ideas for the project,' Neev said, his eyes radiating with the joy he was feeling. His teammates stared at him in surprise.

'We will cut our chart paper in the shape of a chakra, the

Dharma Chakra,' he said. 'We will use pale yellow paper. All the pages will have the same round shape.'

'Fabulous idea,' Rishi said. 'It will suit the theme.'

'I'll draw the Dharma Chakra on the first page,' Akshay volunteered.

Veda nodded.

'We will write the Eight Noble Truths inside the Dharma Chakra,' Neev said. 'Rishi will do that as his handwriting is the neatest.'

Rishi beamed with pleasure.

'Every page will have a Buddhist symbol—a white elephant, a lotus, a deer, a wheel, and so on. Akshay will draw all of them,' Neev continued. 'Just like this exhibition, we will start with the Buddha's birth, narrating the story of the white elephant. That's something which many people may not know.'

'I didn't know about that,' Akshay admitted.

'Neither did I,' Rishi added.

'Tritto,' Veda said.

Neev, too, hadn't known about that aspect of Buddha's life. But he didn't announce it to them.

'When we work on the chapter about the seven lotuses blooming with each step the baby Buddha takes, we will write the different names of Buddha inside each flower,' Neev said, studying their faces. 'Veda will colour the flowers. Her colouring skills are the best amongst us.'

Veda wore a large smile on her face.

'Brilliant idea,' Rishi exclaimed, putting his arm around Neev's shoulder. Akshay thumped him on his back.

Veda stood with her hands on her hips. This was her favourite posture, especially when she wanted to point out something to anyone.

Why is she staring at me? Neev wondered. *Instead of being grateful to me for coming up with such a brilliant idea for the project, she is scowling at me.*

'I'm waiting for you to thank me,' Veda said.

'For what?' Neev countered.

'For dragging you boys to this exhibition. If not for me, this idea would never have popped into your head.'

Neev admitted that she was right. This visit had given him all kinds of amazing ideas that would give NARV's project an edge over the rest of their classmates. Thinking outside of the box had turned out to be a wonderful plan. In fact, it had given them a boxful of unique ideas. And the best part was that Veda hadn't been secretive—none of them were. Unlike him, they openly share resources. This was not just for Project Buddha but even for other class assignments and homework. They were all team players, batting for the team to do well. And Neev would do the same. He would give Team NARV his 120 per cent best.

'Thank you,' he mumbled.

'Louder please, it's not very clear,' she said.

'THANK YOU,' Neev said, startling several people studying the paintings. They watched the children with amusement.

'Now, let's make one more round and spend some more time looking at the paintings,' Veda insisted.

The three boys protested.

'You will find more inspiration,' she said in a voice implying that no further arguments would be accepted.

Reluctantly, the boys started again.

'Our project's last chapter will be each of our learnings from this class assignment,' Rishi said. 'That will add a personalized touch to the assignment and show what the takeaway was for every individual.'

'Super idea,' Neev said. 'Why didn't I think of it?'

'See? Our second round *is* already throwing up more ideas,' Veda smiled.

'Yes, Madam Genius,' Akshay laughed, excited about this new inclusion.

'Our project will be B.O.A.T.' Veda's eyes danced with happiness.

'B.O.A.T.?' Neev looked puzzled. Even Akshay and Rishi were confused.

'Best Of All Times,' she laughed.

The boys shook their heads. This girl was just too much for them to handle.

'We will all leave one by one, with a five-minute interval between each person leaving. It will be just like the way we arrived,' Veda announced. 'Neev will leave last. I'll leave first, then Rishi, followed by Akshay.'

The boys nodded. They wouldn't put it past their classmates to watch their moves or follow them everywhere.

Secrecy was of prime importance here.

8

IN THE LIBRARY

The NARV members were sitting in the school library, several books were open before them. Each one was making notes, which would then go into a folder. From that folder, it would make its way into the actual project.

Neev was poring over a thick book. It had fascinating information about Buddha's early life and his transformation from a prince to a sage. A prince turned ascetic, he was also known as Siddhartha Gautama, Tathagata, and Shakyamuni Buddha. His teachings formed the foundation of Buddhism, the religion he had founded. Neev was surprised to know that the word 'Buddha' meant the 'Awakened One'. It was believed that the sage had

lived for nearly eighty years, and he died near the city of Kushinagar, in northern India. Neev immediately jotted down the entire paragraph.

'Write slowly; that way, your handwriting will improve,' Rishi whispered into his ears.

'Thanks for the reminder,' Neev replied gratefully. He was surprised at the emotions he was feeling. Gratitude. Warmth. A sense of comfort in knowing that someone was trying to help him in a task he found difficult. It was sweet of Rishi to gently remind him about his handwriting. Rishi was climbing the friendship ladder fast, with his genuine warmth and concern. Nowadays, Neev was relaxed around Rishi, not worried about him copying his assignments.

He looked around the spacious library, noticing for the first time the glossiness of the fresh cream paint and the photographs of well-known writers from all over the world on the walls. The school library had undergone a complete renovation a few months back, and now, it looked modern and inviting. Before the revamp, the place had been dull and insipid, with run-down shelves filled with dusty old books.

His classmates sat at different tables, trying to research for their project. There was pin-drop silence. The school's librarian, Miss Meena Mehtani, was extremely particular about students maintaining decorum. She disliked anyone talking or giggling in this sacred space and disturbing others.

'See the way Mihir is staring at us,' Veda whispered. 'He must be hoping that he can borrow the science department's binoculars or the telescope to take a better look at our table.'

Akshay and Rishi laughed. A smile lifted the corners of Neev's lips.

'Silence, please,' Meena Ma'am's voice echoed through the library.

Lowering his head, Neev wrote slowly, filling a page with his cursive writing, which was still a long distance away from being considered neat.

Gautama Buddha was born as Siddhartha in Lumbini, Nepal. His parents were King Shuddhodana and Queen Maya. Scholars say that the Buddha was born in the sixth century bce. It's believed that a seer had predicted that if Prince Siddhartha stayed inside the palace his entire life, he would become a great king. But if he left the palace, he would then become a great religious leader. King Shuddhodana was determined that his son would grow up to become a mighty ruler. He confined Prince Siddhartha inside the palace throughout his childhood so that the seer's prophecy would not come true.

'Just imagine being restricted to a palace because of a prophecy,' Neev said. 'I feel sad for the young boy.'

His friends peered into his notes to read what he had written. When they looked up, they were surprised to see Mihir and his teammates at their table. NARV exchanged worried looks at the way this group had silently crept towards them and caught them unaware.

'Mates, can we borrow a few pens?' Mihir said. The members of his team stood behind him, trying to discreetly peep into NARV's books.

'You are spying on us to see which books we are using for reference,' Neev said accusingly. Placing his arms over the books, he tried to hide their covers.

'Chillax, we just want to borrow a few pens,' Mihir said.

'You walked to the back of the library to borrow our pens? You could have taken them from anyone sitting in the front.' Veda said.

'Sharing is caring,' Akshay said. Gathering a few pens from their table, he handed them to Mihir. 'Don't forget to return them when you are done, and stop trying to peep into our books,' he said.

The moment Mihir and his friends walked away, Veda muttered, 'Those sneaky toads were spying on us, especially Neev.'

'At this rate, we may need a bodyguard for Neev,' Rishi said. 'What if someone kidnaps him and asks for the project as the ransom?'

'Can that happen?' Akshay's eyes widened with fear.

Veda rolled her eyes. Turning to Rishi, she said, 'Your imagination is running away as usual.'

Neev returned to his books. As he wrote furiously, his writing became untidy once again.

One day, while on a chariot ride outside his palace, Prince Siddhartha was deeply tormented by four things that he saw in quick succession: an old man, a sick man, a dead body being carried to its pyre, and a monk meditating under a tree. The four images haunted the young prince to a great extent. He began to reflect upon old age, disease, and death. Leaving behind his royal life and all the luxuries that came with it, Prince Siddhartha followed the path of the monk. He went in search of the cause of suffering, the true nature of the world, and the meaning and purpose of life.

According to Buddhist texts, the Buddha pursued the path of knowledge and is said to have meditated without moving from his seat under a fig tree for seven weeks. To commemorate this feat, a shrine called Animisalocana cetiya was erected in the place where he had sat. After meditating for forty-nine days, the young prince attained enlightenment and found all the answers he was seeking.

A few weeks later, Buddha gave his first sermon at Sarnath. This sermon was called Dhammacakkappavattana Sutta. During this time, he established the monastic order and preached about the Dharma Chakra. Also known as the Wheel of Law, the Dharma Chakra explains the teachings of Buddha and symbolizes Buddhist teachings.

'Read this.' Rishi interrupted Neev and pushed his notebook under Neev's nose.

A pang of envy pricked him as he looked at his teammate's super neat handwriting. *I wish I could write so beautifully*, Neev sighed.

Neev read the paragraph Rishi had just written.

Buddha often spoke about three fires that burnt in a human house. The house was a metaphor for the human body and the fire a metaphor for vices or bad habits, which, if not controlled, destroy a person's peace of mind. The fire or the vices were desire, anger, and delusion. But if these fires were controlled by training the mind spiritually, they had the power to benefit humanity.

'Good job,' Neev said, 'both with the research and the handwriting.'

Rishi's face broke into a pleased grin. Veda and Akshay peered into his notebook, admiring his work.

Staring into the distance, Neev pondered over Buddha's teachings. They were so meaningful. As he flipped the pages of his research notebook, a single thought ran around in his mind. It would be wonderful if he could meet Buddha again. The first visit had been too brief. In fact, it would be great if his teammates, too, could meet Buddha.

Neev continued to read. He came across a passage which said that medieval Buddhist art often depicted the sage giving his first sermon in a deer forest at Sarnath. Sarnath was a pilgrimage site, like Bodhgaya, where the Buddha had attained enlightenment

Turning to another page, Neev read the first paragraph, which mentioned the three jewels or gems of Buddhism: Buddha, Dharma (which means cosmic law and order), and the Sangha (a Sanskrit word that signifies the Buddhist Order or believers of Buddhism, who practise and spread Buddha's teachings). They are often called the Triratna, and anyone who claims devotion to the three gems is said to be a Buddhist.

Buddha believed there is a higher or greater law called 'Dharma' running through the universe and everything in it. By living in accordance with this law, one can attain true wisdom and compassion and, through them, achieve freedom from suffering.

'From what I am reading, I get the feeling that Buddhism is not just a religion. It's a philosophy on living a meaningful and fulfilling life,' Neev turned to his teammates.

'Dude, I have a feeling that we will ace this project,' Akshay said.

Rishi and Veda crossed their fingers.

9

DHARAMJEET

Neev lowered his eyes and flipped the pages of the reference book. He halted at a page with an illustration of a serious-looking young man with an oblong face, whose sharp eyes were focused on the words he was writing. His white dhoti and the white upper cloth wrapped around his left shoulder were spotless. The man's head was devoid of hair, except for a single plait running down the centre of his scalp. Under the flickering light of a mud diya, the man was writing in long scrolls of parchment with an eagle feather. He seemed to be a scholar. A frown marred his broad brow as though he was in deep thought.

Rishi turned to look at the illustration in Neev's book. Then, he returned to his writing.

As Neev watched, the man in the drawing dipped the pointed end of his feather into a mud pot filled with a dark liquid. *It must be my imagination*, Neev thought, blinking his eyes in disbelief. He absentmindedly lifted his school bag and placed it on his lap.

Shaking his head, he continued staring at the page. As Neev traced the outline of the illustration with his finger to check that it was stationary, he felt a sudden pull inside his body. A strong force was jerking him out of his physical body. He held the sides of the table to anchor himself in the library.

The force tugged at him, his grip on the table loosened, and the library disappeared. So did his friends.

Neev found himself standing inside a hut. At his feet was his school bag. It must have slid down from his lap when all the pulling and jerking happened.

He looked up at the lovely dawn sun from a window. It was in a mellow mood, like it had just woken up and was yet to shed its cloak of sleep. The sky was clear of clouds.

'Where am I?' he blinked in surprise when he saw the man in the drawing sitting cross-legged on the ground. The scholar

knitted his eyebrows together; he was probably displeased about something. He rolled up a long parchment. A pot with an eagle feather sat on the floor beside him. The man had just finished writing.

'Have I been transported to another time? How did this happen?' Neev muttered, looking down at his body. He was still in his school uniform, his shirt was a bit wrinkly. A layer of dust coated his black shoes. Just then, Neev realized that there was someone else in the hut, too.

An older man, dressed in a plain white dhoti and a white upper cloth around his left shoulder and with a similar plait running down the centre of his head, sat beside the younger man, watching him with weary eyes. There was an expression of extreme fatigue on his large, pear-shaped face. All the world's tiredness had settled there. The older man was talking to the young scholar.

I hope they can't see me, Neev thought. *I have no idea how people of this time will treat someone from the future*. A bunch of thoughts crossed his mind. Were NARV—actually now it would be ARV as he wasn't in the school library—missing him? Or did they think he had gone to the toilet? Would they peep into his research book? Would they realize how he had disappeared? What would these two scholars think of a boy who had travelled back in time while researching for his school project?

Unmindful of the fact that they had an audience of a curious young boy, the two scholars were engaged in a deep discussion.

'I wish I could understand what they are saying,' Neev muttered.

As a gust of wind swept over him, the two scholars' conversation drifted into Neev's ears. His eyes widened as he realized that he could understand them.

'Dharamjeet,' the older man said, 'you should go to Dhwani. The maharaja of Dhwani presents a question every month. The person who answers the question correctly receives a bag of a hundred gold coins from the king. Our village needs the money, and as the village headman, you should think of the people of the village and not spend time on your interpretation of the scriptures. Your writing won't solve the problems of our people or feed the villagers starving due to the drought that has hit us. But as you are the wisest man in our village, you may just be able to answer the king's question correctly, thereby earning us a bag of gold coins. The people of our village are depending on you.'

Neev stared at the two men.

'My writing isn't going well, Inderjeet-ji,' Dharamjeet said, shaking his head.

'There is a reason your writing isn't going well, Dharamjeet. It's time you put others before yourself,' the older man replied.

Why can't these people see me? Neev wondered. Shuffling his feet noisily, he tried to draw their attention.

Unaware of him standing outside, they continued talking. A slow wind stirred the leaves on the trees. Sparrows flew across the yard.

Neev's eyes widened when he saw a rat near his feet. He jumped, but the rodent, oblivious to his presence, scurried over a couple of old pots stacked one on top of another in the yard. The rat toppled the topmost pot, and it broke the moment it hit the ground.

Both men turned to the entrance of the hut where Neev stood. They looked right through him.

'Must be a rat,' Inderjeet dismissed the disturbance. Turning to his friend, he asked, 'What have you decided?'

Dharamjeet stared into his friend's eyes. 'You are right, Inderjeet-ji,' he nodded. 'I've been selfish for too long. Now, I think it's time I put the villagers' needs before mine.'

'You are young, Dharamjeet; you can complete your interpretation of the scriptures anytime. But your people need you now.' Inderjeet smiled, happy with the knowledge that he had been able to convince his friend. He moved towards the door of the hut.

Neev edged sideways to make way for the older man. Trying to draw attention to himself, he shouted, 'Look at me.'

His voice, like his physical form, didn't exist for the two scholars.

'Now it's time to help your people. Go to Dhwani for the king's question of the month,' Inderjeet said, walking away.

Dharamjeet turned to a woman in a pale yellow sari. She was walking towards him from the corner of the house that doubled as the kitchen. The slim woman had the gentlest eyes Neev had seen. Her long plait ended well below her hips. There was a sheen of perspiration on her face. Her skin glowed, and though she was dressed in simple clothes, she looked radiant.

'Shrimati, I'm going to Dhwani now. It's a day trip. I'll be back by night.'

The woman must be his wife, Neev thought.

Nodding at her husband, the woman darted to the small kitchen. The meal she had cooked was simmering in pots that were over burning logs of wood. Scooping out some food from the pots with a wooden ladle, she wrapped it in two banana leaves. 'Swami, just in case your work may take more than a day, here is some extra food for you,' his wife handed him the packets.

Dharamjeet thanked her and put the parcels into his shoulder bag. Made of a coarse cloth, it was both long and broad. 'Look after yourself and the house,' he said.

He wore his slippers kept outside the doorway. Touching the ground, he started his journey.

Neev was rooted to the spot, unsure about his next move. Should he try to return to school? But how was he supposed to do that? A shiver darted through his body when the thought that what if he was stuck here forever crossed his mind. Had his friends raised an alarm about his disappearance? Taking a couple of calming breaths he made a decision.

'I've no idea why I'm here, but I'll follow Dharamjeet for a while and see what happens,' Neev said, trailing the young scholar.

10

THE PREDICTION

Parched ground stretched before Dharamjeet on all sides. The trees looked dull. The leaves had turned brown. Even the few animals he encountered on the streets looked skeletal, their bones jutting out.

Dharamjeet walked through his village, raising small clouds of dust, unaware that he was being followed by a young boy from the future. As they approached the centre of the village, Neev was surprised to see that it wore the look of a ghostly wasteland. It was so quiet that for a moment, he felt that the villagers had deserted their homes. It looked like a scene straight out of his favourite game: 'Zombies vs Ghosts'.

The handful of huts looked bleak. People were lying on mats inside their houses. They looked sick.

Dharamjeet stood in the centre of the village—his lips pursed and his forehead creased with worry.

'I hope I've not left things for too late,' he muttered. 'With God's grace, I hope I can still save my people from starving to death.' He looked up at a tree where two crows sat on a branch. Neither bird had the energy to caw.

As they walked (Neev staying very close to Dharamjeet), the pleasant morning turned into a hot day. The sun's mood had changed. In the sweltering heat, Dharamjeet constantly wiped his face with his white upper cloth.

Neev looked around curiously as he followed the scholar. Beads of perspiration dribbled down his back, soaking his school uniform. Sweat marbled his upper lip. Adjusting his school bag on his shoulder, he continued walking in Dharamjeet's direction.

The sun was now directly overhead. On his right, he saw the arid riverbed. Cracks criss-crossed across the ground, making patterns that sent shivers rippling down his spine. Neev stepped around the skeletons of a few fish, whose flesh had been picked dry by birds and wild animals.

Soon, Dharamjeet reached the outskirts of the town. A forest stretched out in front of him. He scanned the area, and so did Neev. A large banyan tree, with its thick, leafy branches fanning out in all directions, looked inviting. Dharamjeet sat down under the banyan tree, enjoying the cool shade it provided.

Neev flopped down beside him, watching the scholar as he removed a parcel from his shoulder bag.

With a faraway look on his face, Dharamjeet opened it and ate the rice and vegetables his wife had packed for him. He placed the leftover food under the tree for the birds and insects.

Looking up at a nearby tree, the scholar's eyes shone with happiness. Juicy mangoes dangled from its branches.

'Shrimati loves mangoes,' he said. Picking up several stones, he aimed them at the fruit. His strikes were so accurate that the mangoes dropped easily to the ground. He gathered the fruit in his arms and deposited them in his bag.

As both the journey and the intense heat had tired him, he curled up under the shadiest part of the tree for a short nap. His cloth bag was some distance away.

Neev, too, lay down beside Dharamjeet. Soon, both were sleeping soundly.

Sometime later, Neev was woken up by the rustling of clothes. Rubbing the sleep from his eyes, Neev stared at his surroundings.

Dharamjeet had woken up and was dusting his clothes. Then he picked up his bag, with lines of surprise forming on his face.

'The bag has become a little heavy. Perhaps I plucked too many mangoes,' he muttered. Slinging it over his shoulder, Dharamjeet began walking. Scrambling to his feet, Neev grabbed his school bag and ran behind him, stumbling over the banyan tree's protruding roots.

With a preoccupied look on his face, Dharamjeet continued his journey. He walked through wheat and paddy fields, moving past grazing cows and sheep. A stream gurgled nearby. He stopped to quench his thirst. Neev, too, filled his bottle with water and sipped from it. Then, he refilled the bottle.

Dharamjeet continued walking, reaching the city gates much faster than he had expected. He now stood in Dhwani's crowded market, searching for something. Unlike his village, this place was bustling with life. He looked at the ripe fruit and fresh vegetables in the shops, yearning for the days when his village had boasted of bigger and better vegetables and juicier fruit.

'Hope those days return soon,' Dharamjeet said to himself. His eyes brightened when he found what he was looking for. He moved quickly towards a towering metallic gate richly carved with all kinds of motifs. Behind the gate loomed the large Dhwani palace. With the sun's rays directly over it, the palace glowed like it was made of gold.

Two guards wearing grey dhotis guarded the palace gates. They held long sticks in their right hands. Their bodies were muscular, their legs and hands powerful. The fierce expression on their faces would keep any intruder away.

Can they see me? Neev ran his hand across a guard's arm, expecting a punch to land immediately. Luckily, there was no reaction from the man. Neither did he see the young boy nor feel his touch. *So, no punch*, Neev sighed with relief.

'Looks like I'm invisible to these people, too. Then why am I here?' Neev muttered.

'What is the question for this month?' Dharamjeet asked the guards.

'What can never be bought nor sold, if it's lost, it can never be regained,' the taller guard replied, reading from a scroll. 'Many people are trying to guess the answer to this question.'

'Difficult question, but I'm sure I'll come up with the answer,' Dharamjeet said.

Neev looked puzzled as he mulled over the question. The king had asked a tough question.

'If I hurry up, I can reach my house by sunset and can have dinner with my wife,' Dharamjeet planned. Turning around, he started his journey back to his village, his pace even faster this time.

Neev trailed him, his eyes taking in the sights and sounds of Dhwani. It was a beautiful city with small houses. Many scholars from nearby villages sat under trees pondering over the king's question while the locals went about doing their work. Though attracted by the sights and sounds of the bustling marketplace, Neev constantly looked ahead to keep the scholar in sight.

As Dharamjeet approached the town centre, he saw a sage in white clothes meditating under a tree. Sensing the scholar's presence, the sage opened his eyes. Looking at him intently, he warned Dharamjeet, 'If you return home today, your wife will die. If you don't return, you will die.'

Neev, who was standing directly behind the scholar, moved away to the side. For the briefest of moments, he felt the sage's eyes on him. But the man was indifferent to his presence.

Closing his eyes, the sage once again immersed himself in his meditation. His body went still, and his breathing slowed down.

Dharamjeet's eyes darted all over, wondering whom the sage had addressed. Realizing that he was alone, he stood rooted to the spot. His hands trembled, and his lips quivered. He looked around helplessly, knowing that the sage's prediction could never go wrong.

Neev was startled. What a scary thing for the sage to say. But why had he said that? He thanked his lucky stars that there was no prediction for him. He would have been absolutely devastated, like Dharamjeet. For a second, Neev wished his teammates were with him. He would have loved to discuss this with them. It would have been great to know their thoughts on this.

Dharamjeet waited for the sage to open his eyes and explain what he had meant.

'He will only open his eyes tomorrow morning. By then, it will be too late for you,' an old man standing a little distance away said. He had heard the prediction.

11

MEETING THE BUDDHA AGAIN

Dharamjeet's eyes filled with tears. 'To save my wife from death, I won't go back home today,' he said.

As Neev watched the scholar, an unexplainable sadness overcame him. Though he had met him just a few hours back, he had become fond of the quiet man.

'I'll roam around, waiting for my death,' Dharamjeet said in a choked voice. Tears streamed down his cheeks. His eyes were restless with fear. He even looked up at the sky, perhaps expecting bolts of lightning to strike him.

Dharamjeet cut a sad figure. Bending his head low, he continued walking, taking a different route this time. Neev followed him. As the sun moved to the west, they travelled a long distance, the frown on the scholar's forehead becoming deeper and deeper.

In the distance, in the centre of a clearing, they saw a group of monks in orange robes sitting around a tree. A monk who seemed to be their leader, sat under a large banyan tree, giving a discourse. His hair was piled on top of his head, and he had a peaceful expression on his face. His robes, too, were orange.

As they neared the cluster of monks, the wind carried the head monk's gentle and soothing voice towards them. A deer had stopped in its tracks, watching the sage under the tree. A couple of squirrels sat on the protruding roots of the banyan tree, as if listening to him.

Dharamjeet's eyes widened in surprise. He had recognized the monk.

He was in the presence of Buddha. Though he had never seen him, the description people had given him of the enlightened one matched the man in front of him.

Neev's heart leapt with joy. It was like he was meeting an old friend again.

Quickly wiping his eyes, Dharamjeet sat down behind a group of village folk who had come to hear Buddha's sermon. Neev sat beside him.

A man in grey clothes, wearing a headgear made of shiny spikes and feathers, walked towards them. A monkey trotted beside him. A parrot flew over his head, squawking and screeching. The man had a sharp nose that could cut mangoes, and his chin was so pointed that it could slice a pomegranate. His sharp eyes studied the crowd like an eagle. His long and sleek hair fluttered in the breeze. His beard, too, was long. A cloth bag swung from his shoulder.

As the man approached the gathering, a few villagers had fearful looks on their faces, as if they had seen a ghost. The moment he sat down next to Neev, some of them moved away, whispering furiously to each other.

As Neev moved, he accidentally kept his school bag on the monkey's tail, and the animal turned around to scowl at

him. Its eyes widened, and it tugged its owner's sleeve to draw his attention to the boy.

Can the monkey see me? Neev thought, a chill running over him.

'That's Kalgiya, the sorcerer,' a villager whispered to his group.

Kalgiya turned to his side. His piercing eyes held Neev to the spot. The sorcerer's eyes scanned Neev from head to toe, as though he could see the boy clearly. Neev felt a sharp ripple of fear slice through his body, making him tremble. 'The boy from the future,' Kalgiya said in a low voice. The sorcerer touched Neev's head. Then, he laid his hand on Neev's knee.

Neev felt tremors invade his body. His mouth turned dry, his eyes were wide with apprehension, as he stared at the sorcerer. *What is happening to me?* Neev thought. *Can the sorcerer see me?* Kalgiya had a tattoo of a black circle with three dots inked on his left hand.

Goosebumps erupted on Neev's arms. A tingling sensation started in his legs, travelling to the top of his head where Kalgiya had touched him. A wave of intense heat swept over Neev. He shivered under its impact, feeling a sense of unease. Kalgiya's eyes were wide as he studied the boy.

Buddha's gaze swept over everyone in the gathering. As it rested on Neev, a tide of coolness swept through his body. He stopped trembling and started feeling like his normal self again.

Buddha continued his sermon, occasionally looking at different people in the gathering. But after that initial glance, which Neev now attributed to chance, there was no sign that he had recognized him or even seen him.

'It looks as though I'm invisible to everyone here,' Neev muttered, earning an intense look from the sorcerer.

But this time the sorcerer's look didn't evoke a strong reaction in Neev's body. He just felt a slight tremor in his arms.

The crowd listened to the sermon.

'The four noble truths hold true for all times. All life is suffering. This suffering is caused by irrelevant and meaningless desires that make one's mind restless. There is a way to destroy these desires. A desireless state which frees one from suffering can be attained by following the eightfold path,' Buddha said, looking at the gathering of rapt listeners.

'What is the eightfold path?' a villager asked.

'The principles of the eightfold path are easy to understand and follow. If there is right understanding, right thought, right speech, right conduct, right ways of making a living, right mental attitude devoid of extreme emotions, right mindfulness in all situations, and right concentration, then the eightfold path is attainable,' Buddha replied. 'The eightfold path develops wisdom, morality, and concentration. With the right understanding and the right thoughts comes wisdom. With the right speech, the right action, and the right livelihood, one's character attains morality. With the right effort and mindfulness, one develops concentration. The noble eightfold path leads one from worldly sorrow or samsara to the highest spiritual state of nibbana, which you all call nirvana.'

Neev smiled, he had come across both these words while researching. While 'nirvana' was a Sanskrit word, 'nibbana' was a word in Pali.

'What if one achieves a few aspects of the eightfold path, but not all eight?' a young man asked. 'What is one to do then?'

'The wheel of Dharma or the Dharma Chakra consists of eight spokes, each one of these spokes represents one aspect of this eightfold path,' Buddha explained. 'Even if a single element is missing, the wheel is incomplete. Will an incomplete wheel lead you to your destination, to fulfilment?'

The crowd shook their heads.

Dark clouds had loomed over them. The villagers' eyes frequently strayed to the sky. They hoped it wouldn't rain until they reached their homes.

Only Buddha remained unaffected by the looming storm.

'The cyclical movement of the Dharma Chakra also symbolizes the cyclical nature of life, the ups and downs one experiences, and the ebb and flow one sees. Only if one has the same mental attitude in all situations, can one experience peace and happiness,' Buddha said.

Soon, the dark clouds floated away, and the villagers looked relieved. Buddha had the same calm expression on his face; not for a moment did his expression waver.

'Peace comes from within; do not seek it outside,' Buddha continued. 'Do not dwell in the past; do not dream of the future. Focus on the present moment, as only that moment is yours. The past has gone, the future is yet to unfold.' Closing his eyes, Buddha fell silent, signifying the end of the sermon.

Shutting their eyes, the monks sat in meditation.

Kalgiya moved towards Buddha and prostrated before him.

'O Enlightened One, I've heard so much about you,' he said in his deep voice. 'Please accept my offering.' Reaching into his cloth bag, Kalgiya prostrated before Buddha and placed a small basket at his feet. In it was a cluster of berries.

Several other villagers surrounded Buddha, seeking his advice on several matters. Some of them offered him fruits, vegetables, and flowers; a few others had brought grains and nuts. All these offerings were placed at the sage's feet, next to the berries.

'A monk like me has no requirement for any of these,' Buddha told the crowd, pointing to all the stuff at his feet. 'I request you all to please take whatever you all want from these offerings. I've accepted them with love, and now, want you all to have them.'

As no one could refuse Buddha, the villagers each picked up a fruit, vegetable, nuts, or flower, accepting it as a blessing from the sage. Several drifted away, though a few lingered, reluctant to leave his serene presence. Kalgiya took some nuts and a handful of rice. His monkey lifted a banana. The parrot squawked in protest, making the monkey pick up a guava for him.

Standing up slowly, Dharamjeet made his way towards Buddha.

Prostrating, he beseeched, 'Help me, Enlightened One.'

'What is it, child?' Buddha asked in a gentle voice.

Dharamjeet narrated the meeting with the sage near the village well, telling Buddha about the man's terrible prediction.

Kalgiya watched Buddha with interest, eager to know his reply.

'Only you can save me from death, from that prophecy.' Dharamjeet fell at Buddha's feet.

For some strange reason, the look on the scholar's face reminded Neev of Rishi and Akshay. Biting his lip, he wondered why he had always turned away his classmates when all they wanted to do was be friends with him.

Staring at Dharamjeet, Buddha said in a soft voice, 'I'm feeling very hungry. Do you have something to eat?'

Kalgiya stared at all the food placed before the Enlightened One. So did Neev. It was a strange request.

Though startled at Buddha's question, the scholar sat up when he remembered the dinner his wife had packed for him. The food packet was in his shoulder bag, along with the mangoes he had plucked.

With a smile on his face, he turned to open his bag.

'Please don't open the bag, just hand it to me,' Buddha said.

Dharamjeet did as he was told.

12

THE UNINVITED GUEST INSIDE THE BAG

Accepting Dharamjeet's bag with a calm expression on his face, Buddha put his hand inside and, to everyone's surprise, pulled out a small snake. The monks recoiled at the sight of the deadly snake. Kalgiya's eyes widened, and he turned to Buddha. A slew of emotions—respect, admiration, awe, and envy—hovered on his face for several moments before they drifted away.

The reptile lay in Buddha's hand, as still as a rope. The moment the Enlightened One lowered the animal to the ground, it slithered away into the bushes, startling the squirrels and making them scamper up the tree quickly.

Dharamjeet now understood what had happened. 'I remember plucking some mangoes and dropping them into

the bag after I had removed my lunch from it. Then I kept it aside and went to sleep. The snake must have crawled inside it. By carrying the bag on my shoulder, I have been carrying death all along on this journey because a poisonous snake was hidden inside it.' Tears flowed down his cheeks.

'At this point, I feel lucky that I'm invisible to everyone,' Neev muttered. 'I can't believe that I was walking so close to the snake all this time!'

'If I had returned home, I would have handed the bag to my wife. My unsuspecting wife would have put her hand into it to remove my food and the mangoes. She would then have been stung to death by the snake,' Dharamjeet said. 'And if I hadn't gone home, then the snake would have bitten me when I would open the bag to take out my dinner.'

A sudden thought struck Neev. *Was an uninvited guest like that snake sitting inside his school bag*?

'Nah,' he muttered. 'If I'm invisible to everyone in this time, so is my bag. But I better not take any chances.'

Dropping his bag to the ground, he slid the zipper open. 'If there is any intruder inside, it will slither out.' He watched the bag for some time. But nothing emerged from its depths. Seeing a couple of ants crawl towards his bag, he hastily lifted it.

Dharamjeet again fell at Buddha's feet, weeping tears of joy.

'It's getting late, Dharamjeet,' Buddha urged. 'You have a long distance to travel. Make haste.'

It was Dharamjeet's good fortune that had led him to Buddha. He marvelled at how the Enlightened One, the all-knowing monk, had saved him from a disastrous fate.

'Don't waste time, Dharamjeet. Time is precious, and your wife and the people of your village are waiting for you,' Buddha said. 'Save your people first, the rest can come later.'

The sage's words were imbued with great meaning.

Dharamjeet stood up, nodding as though he had understood the hidden value of the sage's words. Next, he pulled four mangoes from his bag and placed them at Buddha's feet. Afterward, he scooped up a handful of nuts and rice, dropping them into his bag. Suddenly, he picked up an orange and added it to the contents of his bag.

Wiping his tears, he turned around and started walking towards the direction of his village. He had a quickness and a spring in his stride that had been missing this morning. The perpetual frown had cleared from his brow.

The small gathering of people still clustered around Buddha sat in silence for some time, assimilating what had happened to Dharamjeet.

'Aren't you going to talk to me, Neev?' Buddha looked straight at the young boy who had now stood up. 'How is your school project coming along?'

'You can see me? Why couldn't Dharamjeet or any of the other people I met see me?' Neev asked. Gesturing to the monks, who were all looking around with confused expressions and wondering who Buddha was conversing with, Neev said, 'Even the monks can't see me.'

'They can't see you as you don't belong to their time,' Buddha said. 'You are so far ahead in the distant future that at this moment, you are a speck somewhere in the universe.'

'But you can see me?' Neev asked.

Buddha smiled.

'Is it because the past, present, and future are all a play for you?' Neev asked as he walked towards Buddha.

The sage smiled again. He had the kindest eyes Neev had ever seen in his life. Eyes that brought peace and happiness. 'If they can't see me, how am I able to understand their language?' Neev asked. 'I read in one of the books that people of this time spoke Magadhi Prakrit and Pali. I don't know both these languages.'

'Neev, when you were standing at Dharamjeet's doorstep, you were presented with two choices. Either you would become visible to the people of the past, or you would be able to understand what they were speaking,' Buddha replied. 'Your subconscious desire that you wished you could understand their language manifested as your thought, which in turn became your choice. You chose to be able to understand what everyone was speaking rather than be seen by them.'

'So, it was my choice?' Neev asked.

'Yes.'

'But I think that sorcerer can see me, like the sage who made that prediction for Dharamjeet,' Neev said in a lowered voice.

'Some people have that ability,' Buddha replied, but he didn't elaborate further.

'What do I call you?' Neev asked.

'Whatever your heart desires, whatever makes you happy,' Buddha replied.

'Why do sages always meditate under trees?' he asked, looking up at the dense foliage of the banyan tree.

'Trees are so selfless, Neev. They give the best parts of themselves so wholeheartedly, expecting nothing in return. By meditating under something so noble, one receives only pure vibrations,' Buddha answered.

'True,' Neev nodded. 'Our school has asked us to plant trees on our birthdays.'

'That's such a wonderful idea,' Buddha smiled. 'Your time needs the selflessness of trees more than ever. Trees not just provide food for other creatures, they also house several insects, birds, and animals.'

Kalgiya, who had been listening to Neev and Buddha's conversation till now, was forced into getting up and moving away as his pets had got into a fight with some eagles.

'What is the answer to the king's question?' Neev looked puzzled. 'What can never be bought nor sold, and if it is lost, can never be regained?'

'The answer is so simple, Neev,' Buddha smiled. 'Don't tell me that the class topper hasn't been able to guess the answer?'

'It's such a difficult and tricky question,' Neev replied, frowning. He thought for a while and said, 'Is it time?'

'Yes, the answer is time, Neev,' Buddha said with a wise smile. 'Time can neither be bought nor sold. Once time is lost, it can never be regained. The answer is so relevant to Dharamjeet. On the pretext of writing his interpretation of the scriptures, he ignored his duties and responsibilities as the village headman. The time he wasted could have been better used to serve the villagers who rely on him for every small and big requirement. Dharamjeet's life has a purpose, which he has neither realized nor is he even close to fulfilling.'

'Is that the reason you saved him from the snake bite?' Neev asked.

'Yes,' Buddha nodded. 'He is yet to fulfil his purpose in life.'

'Why am I here?' Neev asked again.

'To meet me,' Buddha laughed. 'You were yearning to see me again as you had several secrets you wanted to share with me.'

13

LIVE IN THE MOMENT

Neev was silent. He had wanted to meet Buddha again. During their last meeting, he had felt so shy in the great sage's presence that all the things he wanted to discuss had been left on the tip of his tongue and then duly swallowed.

'So, Neev, tell me the things lying on the tip of your tongue,' Buddha's eyes twinkled.

Neev's eyes widened. Buddha had voiced aloud his exact thoughts.

'I'm a part of NARV now,' he blurted out, explaining about the project, what NARV was and how he had tried his best to get out of it but hadn't been able to. 'We are all doing the project together.'

'Are you enjoying working with them?' Buddha asked.

'They are growing on me,' Neev said. 'You were right. Some journeys aren't meant to be taken alone.'

'Why were you so hesitant earlier?' Buddha smiled.

'I'm scared that they will sneak my secrets to everyone.'

'What secrets?'

'That my parents are divorced.' As he said those words, tears rolled out from Neev's eyes. 'That I am so confused and worried and feel sad about it.'

'Veda already knows about it,' Buddha said. 'Has she told anyone?'

Neev shook his head. 'I was surprised that she hasn't yet revealed it to Akshay and Rishi.'

'She must be waiting for you to do that as it's your secret. Why should she share it with others?'

'That makes sense,' Neev nodded.

'Neev, the answer to the king's question is relevant to you as much as it is to Dharamjeet,' Buddha said gently. 'You are wasting your time blaming your mother for your parents' divorce, making her feel guilty. She is suffering as much as you are. Your mother is a good woman, and your father is a good man. But when two people are unhappy in a relationship, they decide to keep away rather than make each other miserable. It's just that, that particular decision to live separately was made by your mother. Someone had to take that step. Enjoy the time with your mother. She has sacrificed a lot for you and is trying very hard to keep you happy.'

A strange sadness engulfed Neev when Buddha mentioned his father.

'Neev, you are spending too much time in the past, always reliving the good times you had when your parents were together. You are also frequently dreaming about your parents getting back together. Such thoughts are taking away the joy from your present. The present is the most important moment in time—it is both here and now. The past and the future are irrelevant; one is gone, and the other is yet to come,' Buddha said. 'When you live in the moment, you can make the most of whatever time you spend with your parents. The only thing you should retain from the past is the lessons you learned from it.'

Neev wiped his wet eyes with the back of his palm.

'Every Sunday, I used to play football with a group of boys and their fathers,' Neev said. 'Now Dad has left us, and I can't play football.'

'You can always ask your mother to join you,' Buddha said. 'You are living in a time when women are achieving impossible feats. Football is just a game. Your mother will happily join you every Sunday. She wants to spend as much time as she can with you. Just give her a chance.'

Neev was silent.

'And give your teammates a chance, Neev. They really want to be your friend, and you very much need good friends in your life. And because of this project, you will have three great companions at once! Such friends will help you navigate the emotional lows you are facing,' Buddha said.

Neev felt Kalgiya's eyes on him. The same tingling sensation arose within him.

'Why can Kalgiya see me and not anyone else?' he asked again.

'He has acquired some *siddhis* with his magic, and with these traits, he can see and touch you.'

Neev turned around to look at the sorcerer. Kalgiya had been trying to save his pets from the eagles intent on pecking the monkey and the parrot. Neev's eyes widened when he saw that in place of the eagles, there were now a few rats with funny coloured tails. So, the sorcerer had transformed the birds who were troubling his pets into rodents. Scared of Kalgiya's powers, Neev fixed his gaze on Buddha and watched him for several moments.

'Neev, can I trust you with a responsibility?' Buddha asked, taking Neev by surprise. 'Please follow the scholar and ensure that the gold coins he earns from the king of Dhwani safely reach home with him. That village needs the money. Don't leave Dharamjeet alone even for a single moment.'

'But Dharamjeet must be on his way to his village. How will I catch up with him?' Neev asked.

'Seeing the crowd of scholars in Dhwani, all eager to come up with the answer to the king's question, he has changed his mind about heading to his village tonight. He is going back to Dhwani to give his answer. You will find him on that path,' Buddha pointed to his right. 'Go quickly, you can catch up with him. Before you leave, do take whatever you want from these,' Buddha pointed to all the things the villagers had offered him.

Neev noticed a few vegetables he disliked eating. As his eyes fell on the cluster of berries, he picked it up. Berries were his favourite.

A couple of villagers still sitting behind the monks gasped

as the berries floated in the air. They couldn't see Neev and were confounded about who had lifted those berries from the offerings at Buddha's feet.

'That's the sorcerer's offering,' someone in the gathering whispered.

Neev stiffened. There was no way he was picking up Kalgiya's offering.

'Good choice, Neev, ' Buddha said approvingly. 'They will help you when you need them the most. Eat it not when you are hungry, but when you require assistance.'

'How will I know when to eat the berries?' Neev asked.

'Your intuition will guide you,' Buddha replied. 'Like Dharamjeet, your time in this world of the past has a purpose which you must fulfil. And don't worry if your invisibility doesn't last and you become visible to some people.'

Neev's eyes widened. *Was that a warning?*

14
THE ANSWER TO THE KING'S QUESTION

Neev dropped the berries into his school bag. Carrying the bag on his shoulder, he started running in the direction Buddha had pointed. Dharamjeet was nowhere to be seen. Panting heavily, Neev stood on the path, looking all around and catching his breath.

'I wish I had Akshay's stamina,' he muttered. 'By now, he would have caught up with Dharamjeet.'

After several seconds, he once again started running on the path. His eyes gleamed when he saw Dharamjeet walking ahead briskly.

Catching up with him, Neev deliberately slowed down his steps. He was now behind the scholar, just by a few feet.

The sun was starting to set. Bird calls filled the air. A cool breeze moved about lazily, stirring the leaves on the trees and making their clothes flutter. A few cowherds were taking their cows back home after grazing.

Dharamjeet, closely followed by Neev, continued walking at a brisk pace until they reached the bustling market. Dharamjeet made his way towards the massive entrance of the palace.

'I must give my answer to the king quickly,' he told the men guarding the gates.

'It's late now. Come back in the morning,' one guard said.

At that moment, a member of the royal staff walked towards the duo. 'Don't you two ever listen?' he asked, irritated.

'The maharaja has specifically instructed that anyone who requests an audience with him regarding the answer to the question should be sent inside the palace immediately. The only exception is when the king is sleeping. Then the person should be escorted to the guest room to spend the night, and he or she can meet the king first thing the next morning.'

The two guards exchanged alarmed looks. They had missed the king's instructions. If not for their friend, they would have made a mistake. If the king had come to know about their error, it would have got them into deep trouble.

'*Kshama, Mahashaya,*' they apologized. Opening the gates, they allowed Dharamjeet into the palace. Neev quickly darted through the gap, close behind the scholar.

The third guard escorted Dharamjeet into the palace. Neev's eyes widened at the opulence of the corridors they passed through. The floor was shiny, the walls were adorned with paintings of the previous kings and queens, and the massive pillars were carved with an array of sculptures painted in dark hues. The large windows, letting in ample light, had carvings of birds and animals.

They halted inside the large central court. Luckily for them, the king was conducting a meeting with his ministers and the head of his army. Seeing the newcomers, he held up his hand to silence a minister speaking in whispers.

'What can I do for you, *Mahashaya*?' he asked Dharamjeet.

Neev observed the king. He looked young. He was tall and muscular, as though he exercised a lot, and had shoulder length hair. Dressed in a bright red dhoti, gold ornaments glittering on his chest, and a crown of jewels on his head, he watched them with a gentle look in his eyes. His features were as perfect as a painting. Large rings adorned his slim and long fingers. An *angavastram* with gold motifs was draped across one shoulder. On his feet were ornamental slippers. *He must be in his early twenties*, Neev thought.

Bowing deeply before the king, his palms joined in a *pranam*, Dharamjeet said, 'I would like to answer the question of the month.'

King Veersara smiled. He loved the company of wise men. He gestured to Dharamjeet to come closer. The ministers watched the scholar with curious eyes. He was the first man to attempt the answer to the question that had been announced just a few hours ago. So far, no one else had come forward as everyone liked to mull over the answer.

Taking the king's nod as permission to speak, Dharamjeet said, 'Respected Maharaj, the answer is time.'

The king's face split into a huge smile. He clapped his hands. 'This is the first time someone has answered a question so quickly.'

The *raj darbar* broke into a thunderous applause. Neev, too, joined in. Maharaja Veersara summoned a minister and whispered something into his ears.

Neev stared at the minister, wondering where he had seen him. His sharp features and sleek hair looked familiar. The minister disappeared into one of the passageways along the court. There was silence as everyone waited for the man to return. Several minutes later, the minister walked into the *raj darbar*, carrying a large bag in his left hand.

The first thing Neev noticed was a black tattoo in the shape of a circle with three dots on the minister's left hand.

Must be a popular tattoo of these times, Neev thought. *Though simple, the design looks scary.*

Approaching the king, the minister pulled open the drawstring of the bag and showed the maharaja the contents.

Then he shook it. The coins jingled and jangled. Lifting the bag from his minister's hands, the king gestured to Dharamjeet to come forward. As the scholar neared, the king handed the bag to him. 'Because you answered so fast, I have added fifty more coins to the original prize of a hundred,' the king said.

'Thank you, Maharaj, your generosity is unparalleled. I had heard so much about it, now I have experienced it.' Tears rolled down Dharamjeet's face as he clutched the bag of coins close to his chest. The people of his village would be overjoyed at this bounty.

The minister whispered something in Maharaja Veersara's ear. The king smiled and nodded.

Turning to Dharamjeet, he said, 'I insist that you spend the night in one of the guest rooms in the palace as it will be too risky for you to head towards your village after dusk. Please accept our hospitality and stay here for the night. Food will be served to you in your room.'

Neev beamed as though the king had invited him personally. This was extremely thoughtful of the maharaja, and Neev liked such people.

'Your wish is my command, Maharaja. I'm honoured and privileged that you consider me worthy of your hospitality,' Dharamjeet said.

'Scholars have always been close to my family's heart,' King Veersara replied. 'It's an honour that we can host you in our palace.'

'Mahamantri, please escort him to the guest room and take care of all his needs,' the king instructed the minister who had bought the bag of coins.

Dharamjeet and Neev walked with the mahamantri down several passages, each one taking them further and further away from the court. Thanks to his excellent memory, Neev had memorized the route. It was now engraved into his brain. Honestly, it was quite easy as they constantly turned to the right.

Opening a door to a large room, the mahamantri said, 'Please rest here for the night. Your food will be brought to you shortly.'

As Dharamjeet and Neev entered the room, the minister shut the door and walked back to the court.

'This is so easy-peasy,' Neev grinned. 'Tomorrow, Dharamjeet will be back in his village, and I will be back in my school library.'

15

CAUGHT AND THROWN IN THE DUNGEON

Neev looked around. Two lamps illuminated the room. A mud diya was placed near the bed.

A large bed covered with a red velvet bedsheet and several small pillows occupied most of the room. The bed looked comfortable and could easily hold four adults. Walking towards it, he sat down.

In a corner of the room, several mats were rolled up. Heading towards them, Dharamjeet lifted one mat made of coconut fibre and spread it open beside the bed. Neev immediately moved his feet away.

Several minutes later, two boys wearing light-coloured dhotis and *angavastrams* entered the room, carrying two big *thalis* covered with banana leaves. They placed the *thalis* before the scholar. As they lifted the banana leaves, Neev saw that one *thali* was filled with food. The other *thali* had a tumbler of water, desserts, and some fruit.

'Please eat,' one boy said, joining his palms. It looked as though he was in his mid-teens. 'If you want more, do let me know.'

'Thank you. This will be sufficient,' Dharamjeet said politely. 'You work in the kitchen?' he asked the boys.

'We are the cook's helpers,' the boy said. 'My name is Tara, and this is Chand, my younger brother.'

Dharamjeet smiled at the boys.

'The king is leaving now,' Tara said by way of a conversation.

Dharamjeet frowned. 'Where to?' he asked.

'To Samsa, the next kingdom. The king is our Maharaja Veersara's friend. Sadly, Samsa has been attacked by the Dakawis. The king just received a message through a pigeon, and he is summoning the cavalry right now. Everyone is going. Only the mahamantri will be in the palace with a few others.'

'You are lucky that you met the king today. If you had been even an hour late, you would not have met the maharaja as he would have left the palace by then,' Chand explained.

'*Mahashaya*, please eat, we will collect the empty plates later,' Tara said politely.

The two brothers left the room, closing the door softly behind them.

Taking the tumbler, Dharamjeet filled his palm with water and sprinkled it all around the *thali*. Then, with hands joined together, he said a prayer. Removing half the food into a *thali*, he covered it with a banana leaf. Dharamjeet slowly ate the portion he had separated from the main *thali*.

Once his meal was over, he washed his hands in the *thali* and lay down on the mat instead of the opulent bed in the guest room.

Intense pangs of hunger gnawed at Neev's stomach. It was several hours since he had eaten breakfast. As he had forgotten his lunch box at home, there was nothing in his backpack that he could eat. He eyed the food eagerly. 'If I eat from that *thali*, will I be stealing?' he asked himself. 'But as I am on a mission set by Buddha himself, I think I can at least eat something. I am sure Buddha wouldn't want me to starve.'

Removing the banana leaf, he sat down crossed-legged on the floor and started eating. The food was delicious, though loaded with ghee. Neev gulped down the *katori* of kheer. Its taste was out of this world.

Keeping some savoury snacks inside his pocket for emergency munching, he pulled a mattress from the stack in the corner of the room. Spreading it beside Dharamjeet's, he lay down. The scholar was fast asleep.

'I'm lucky that Dharamjeet doesn't snore,' Neev remarked. 'The worst roommate one can have is a snoring one.'

His eyelids drooped. Soon, sleep washed over Neev.

Sometime later, he heard the door creak open.

Neev sat up straight, instantly alert. Rubbing the sleep out of his eyes, he stared

at the door. In the soft glow of the lamp flames and the moonlight streaming through the window, he saw the minister who had given Dharamjeet the bag of gold coins standing at the threshold of the large room.

'Why is the mahamantri inside this room at this time in the night?' Neev whispered to himself. 'There is something odd about it.'

As Neev watched, the mahamantri crept towards

Dharamjeet's brown bag lying beside him. Opening it, the man silently removed the pouch of gold coins from it. Holding it close to his chest, he turned to leave the room.

'Don't steal the bag.' Neev stood up and grabbed hold of the mahamantri's arm. The tingling was back in his body.

The mahamantri veered around at the sound of Neev's voice. His eyes widened when he saw the young boy standing on the mat beside the sleeping Dharamjeet. His eyes studied Neev from top to bottom.

'Who are you?' he asked. 'What are you doing in the room with this scholar?'

Before Neev could reply, Dharamjeet woke up. He was taken aback seeing the young boy standing beside him.

'Who are you?' Dharamjeet stuttered.

'I'll tell you later,' Neev said. 'First, we have to catch this thief,' he pointed to the mahamantri clutching the bag of coins.

'How dare you call me a thief?' the mahamantri thundered. 'I'm sure you and this scholar are our enemies who have gained entry into the palace. This man is only pretending to be a scholar. Guards, come here quickly,' the mahamantri screamed.

They heard thundering feet as several men in grey dhotis and carrying long sticks in their arms rushed into the room.

'Only one man, this scholar, had presented himself in the *raj darbar* earlier this evening. But now, there are two of them,' he said. 'Their timing is so suspicious. They arrived on the eve of the king's departure. Everyone knew that the king was ready to leave at a moment's notice. They are up to something. See how oddly this boy is dressed. Even his hair looks peculiar. Lock them up in the dungeons.'

The guards marched a shocked Neev and a devastated Dharamjeet out of the room, taking them through unending passageways. They went down several floors and reached the dungeons, far below the palace.

Unfortunately, Neev couldn't grab his school bag and Dharamjeet's brown bag before they were dragged out.

They were thrown into a cellar, and the thick iron door with grilles locked. When the guards left, the two stared at each other in dismay.

'Who are you?' Dharamjeet once again asked Neev.

Neev narrated the entire sequence of events, from his school project to meeting Buddha for the first time to following Dharamjeet to the time they were caught. As he spoke, the panic and worry began dissipating from the scholar's face.

'You are from the future? You have come to help me?' Dharamjeet said, as though he was talking to himself.

'Not too sure about the help part,' Neev replied, staring at the dungeon.

'I'm sure if Buddha chose you to escort me to my village, he must have seen some capability in you,' Dharamjeet said softly. He sat down on the stone floor. In contrast to the rich palace, the dungeon was dingy and dark.

Neev paced about the dungeon, cursing himself for his stupidity. *This is not easy-peasy.*

'I wish Akshay, Rishi, and Veda were here to help me. I'm sure with their assistance I would have got out of this situation,' he said, tracing the words 'help me' on the dungeon wall with his forefinger.

16

THE ARU OF NARU

'Haven't my teammates realized that I have disappeared from the library?' Neev grumbled. 'If I'm stuck in the dungeon forever, then they can say goodbye to the project. No way will they win without me.'

'Overconfidence isn't a good thing, Neev,' Veda said.

'And talking to yourself is indeed a sign of madness,' Akshay added.

'What are you doing in a dungeon?' Rishi asked, the only one with concern in his voice.

Neev was startled. *Am I hearing voices? Am I going crazy?*

He stared in disbelief. His teammates were standing outside the dungeon, peering at Dharamjeet and Neev through the bars. The scholar's mouth fell open as he watched the three children standing outside the dungeon. He turned to Neev with questions in his eyes.

Neev pinched himself to check if he was dreaming. *The ARV of NARV were here!*

'Ouch,' Veda said. 'That must have hurt.'

No, he wasn't dreaming. His friends were here!

He rushed towards them. He had never been happier to see them. Like him, they were also in their school uniforms and just like him, Veda had her school bag with her.

'How did you all reach here?' Neev asked.

'We took a flight and followed you here,' Veda grinned. 'But it was a bumpy ride due to bad weather,' she rubbed her stomach.

Neev shook his head. Whichever time Veda inhabited, she kept her sense of humour intact. That was a good thing. If she had her wits around her, she could probably save him.

'Tell us how you landed up here!' Rishi said.

For the second time, Neev narrated the sequence of events. He then introduced his friends to Dharamjeet. The scholar had dropped the shocked expression from his face when he realized that the new entrants were Neev's friends. He greeted them warmly. The children reciprocated the warmth.

'But Neev, something must have broken your shield of invisibility and made you visible to the mahamantri when you grabbed his hand,' Akshay said thoughtfully. 'You mentioned that you heard the sorcerer call you the "boy from the future". So, that means even he and his pets could see you.'

'That's not important now,' Veda said. 'We need to think how to get them out from here,' she gestured to Neev and Dharamjeet.

'How did you all end up here?' Neev asked again. 'But it's a good thing that you all are not invisible.'

'After you suddenly disappeared from the library, we waited for some time, thinking that you must have gone to the restroom,' Veda said.

'A little later, I went hunting for you in the washrooms,' Akshay added. 'But you weren't there.'

'I went back to the classroom looking for you,' Rishi joined in.

'When I searched your seat for clues, I realized that your school bag was missing. That's when I got suspicious,' Veda said.

'But it was Rishi who put two and two together,' Akshay said. He was staring at Dharamjeet.

The scholar was listening to their conversation.

'When I peeped into your book while you were reading, I clearly remember seeing Dharamjeet sitting and writing in that sketch. But when I looked at the same drawing again, he was sitting inside a dark room, looking helpless and sad,' Rishi joined the conversation. 'The sudden change in the sketch made me very suspicious.'

Dharamjeet's eyes widened when he heard about his sketch in the book.

Neev stared at Rishi, thinking of all the times he had snubbed his offers of getting to know each other.

'I studied the new sketch. What stunned me was the words "help me" in your handwriting on the wall…inside the picture,' Rishi continued.

Neev's eyes widened with shock. The words he had scrawled with his finger had ended up in the sketch in the book, and those words had brought his friends to his rescue.

'Veda was the first to touch the drawing, then she disappeared. At that time, we realized we were on the right track,' Rishi said. 'Then it was Akshay's turn, and finally mine.'

'I grabbed my bag with one hand and traced Dharamjeet's outline with the other hand,' Veda explained. 'That was my boarding pass for time travel.'

'Can you all do me a favour?' Neev asked.

'Dude, we are here to do you lots of favours,' Veda said.

'I left my school bag in the guest room. Even Dharamjeet's brown bag is there. Could you please get it for us?'

'Not an easy task,' Akshay said. 'We may get lost in this palace and never find you.'

'Have no fear when Veda is here,' she said with a smile.

'What do you have up your sleeve?' Rishi asked.

'Just my arm,' she grinned. 'I have my favourite blue marker. I can keep marking the walls as we move through the palace and find the guest room.'

'You will spoil this beautiful palace with your markers?' Neev countered.

'The housekeeping staff can always wipe it off with soap and water,' she replied, blowing a bubble with her chewing gum.

Dharamjeet watched her in fascination.

'I don't think soap exists in this world, Veda. I think you've forgotten that we've travelled back in time,' Rishi said sarcastically.

'Stop nitpicking about stains on the walls,' she made a face. 'Focus on the larger picture, that is, getting Neev and the scholar out of here.'

Akshay was looking around. 'Looks like you guys aren't important prisoners,' he remarked. 'There is no one guarding the dungeons.'

'That's a good thing, isn't it?' Rishi asked. 'Else, instead of two people behind bars, by now, there would have been five.'

'The palace is short-staffed. Everyone has gone to Samsa, the neighbouring kingdom, to help that king fight the Dakawis,' Neev explained.

'By the time you all stop arguing and worrying about unimportant stuff, Mihir and his teammates would have submitted the project and won the prize,' Veda said.

At the mention of the prize, the boys fell silent.

All this while Dharamjeet had been a silent spectator,

listening to the four children arguing.

'I think this little girl is right. You need to retrieve our bags,' he said.

'This little girl is also a terror,' Rishi added. A stern look from Veda made him swallow his next lot of words.

'See this,' Neev pointed to a line of ants. 'I had dropped a trail of snacks while I was being dragged to the dungeons. The ants will lead you to the room.'

'But once they finish their buffet, then what?' Veda raised her eyebrows. 'Then we will be lost in this *bhool bhulaiya*.'

'Point,' Rishi said. 'You have any ideas?'

'Watch me,' she said.

The boys made puking faces as Veda removed the chewing gum from her mouth. Tearing a bit from the large wad, she popped the remaining into her mouth. Rolling the small piece into a ball, she stuck it near the dungeon wall. Then, she opened her school bag and pulled out her knitting yarn.

'You guys are lucky that I had my knitting classes today.' Veda unravelled the yarn, sticking the loose end over the chewing gum. 'You all have to buy me a new yarn,' she said.

'Sure,' Neev replied. 'Just get us out of here.'

Dharamjeet watched open-mouthed as Veda went about her business.

'This little girl is extremely clever,' he said with awe in his voice.

'Unhygienic, too,' Akshay muttered.

Neev watched his friends leave the dungeon, Veda sticking the yarn to the wall at regular intervals with her chewing gum.

Neev and Dharamjeet sat down facing each other. With nothing else to do, both nodded off to sleep, relaxed that they would soon be rescued.

17

THE STRANGE BERRIES

It was quiet for a while before Akshay, Veda, and Rishi returned. Neev heard their voices before he saw them.

The three were engaged in a heated discussion. Maybe they were arguing.

Dharamjeet's eyes brightened when he saw his brown bag in Rishi's hands. Akshay clutched Neev's school bag.

The two boys dropped the bags close to the door of the dungeon. Inserting his hand through the bars, Neev quickly opened his bag and removed the cluster of berries he had taken from the offerings the people had given Buddha. He had already taken Dharamjeet into confidence and disclosed his plan. The scholar had immediately agreed. The sage's words raced through his mind like wild horses. 'Eat the berries not when you are hungry but when you need help. Your intuition will guide you.'

Neev's inner voice was telling him that the time to eat the berries was now. He dropped one into Dharamjeet's palm and held a berry between his thumb and forefinger, studying it.

He turned towards the scholar. 'At the same time?' Neev asked.

Dharamjeet nodded.

His teammates watched as Neev and Dharamjeet popped the small fruit into their mouths at the same time.

For several seconds, nothing happened. They didn't feel anything different either. Neev was disappointed. He had hoped that the berries would somehow be instrumental in getting him and Dharamjeet out of the dungeon. Perhaps he had hoped that the dungeon grilles would miraculously melt, allowing them a passage out of this prison.

Neev's friends' faces fell. They exchanged worried looks.

Suddenly, Neev and Dharamjeet started shrinking as if they were inflated humans and someone had poked a pin into them. It seemed like all the muscle, bones, and air was leaving their body.

'Dude, you're shrinking!' Rishi looked alarmed.

Akshay stood stiffly, his expression full of panic.

Only Veda looked pleased, a smile spreading on her face as if she had just received an unexpected gift.

'Wonderful,' she said, rubbing her hands in glee.

The other two boys turned to her in surprise.

She continued watching the shrinking Dharamjeet and Neev. They were now the size of a finger.

Veda unzipped her school bag and pulled out a long ruler.

'Are you going to hit them?' Rishi asked, his eyes filling with tears.

'Watch,' she said, bending down. Then she inserted the ruler through the grille.

The thumb-sized Neev quickly grabbed the edge of the ruler tightly with both hands, and Veda pulled him out with ease.

'Genius,' Akshay said.

He lifted Neev and placed him on his palm. Mini Neev constantly fidgeted, moving all over the palm. 'I like this small version,' Akshay grinned. 'I can carry him around and make him do all my homework. He can even help me during exams.'

Neev glared and showed his fist.

'I'm scared,' Akshay laughed.

Veda brought Dharamjeet out the same way and gently placed him on Akshay's palm. Unlike their teammate, the scholar stood still.

Plucking two berries from the cluster in Neev's bag, she gave them to Akshay.

'Now feed them the berries. Make sure they eat it properly, as we want them to return to their normal size, not a few inches shorter,' she ordered.

'Yes, Ma'am,' Akshay said.

He held the berries close to Neev and Dharamjeet's lips. Both were unable to take the fruit into their mouths. It was difficult to hold the fruit in their extra small hands, and their tiny mouths could not bite in the berries.

'This isn't working,' Rishi said tearfully.

They were losing hope.

'Hold the berries close to their mouths and let them lick it,' Veda instructed.

Neev and Dharamjeet started licking the fruit. Their tiny tongues darted out, touching the fruit, yet their size remained small.

Rishi, Veda, and Akshay exchanged frustrated looks.

'I'm sure Neev's mom would like her son back in his normal size, not this teeny-weeny one,' Veda remarked, chewing her lower lip nervously.

Veda gasped with surprise when she noticed that with each subsequent lick, Neev and Dharamjeet were gaining strength. Then, with tremendous effort, they took small bites of the fruit. Slowly, their size started increasing. Their friends looked relieved.

Akshay quickly deposited the two to the ground. The three of them held their breaths and watched Neev and Dharamjeet. As their bodies increased in size, they became stronger and gained the ability to chew faster and better. Little by little, they expanded in height and breadth.

Within a few minutes, Neev and Dharamjeet were back to their normal size.

'Feeling OK?' Veda asked.

Dharamjeet and Neev nodded. Then both looked at their hands and feet, watching them as if they were seeing their limbs for the first time.

'Mission Back to Normal accomplished,' Veda said.

'Thank you, children,' Dharamjeet said in a voice quivering with emotion.

'Thank you, friends. I owe you all a treat,' Neev added.

'Just get us the prize,' Akshay grinned.

'First, we need to get Dharamjeet his coins back,' Neev announced.

His friends exchanged grins. They were enjoying this adventure.

'We are ready,' Veda said.

18

THE SORCERER

'Let's go back to the room in which you two stayed for a few hours,' Veda suggested. 'No one will look for us there.'

Following Veda's chewing gum and knitting yarn trail, the motley group reached the guest room. Everything was the same as they had left it.

They all sat down—some on the mats, a few on the bed—staring at each other in silence, perhaps wondering what the next course of action would be.

'I want to tell you all a secret,' Neev said. He wanted to unburden himself as carrying it within himself was giving him a tummy ache.

All eyes turned to him.

'My parents have divorced,' he said quickly, lowering his head as though he was staring at something on the ground.

'I already know that,' Veda replied.

'Dude, my parents have been divorced for two years,' Rishi admitted in a soft voice. 'I've survived it. So will you.'

Neev was taken aback. He turned to look at his teammate. Rishi was so normal, his grades high, and his behaviour towards everyone so pleasant. That meant that Rishi had handled his parents' separation quite well and still maintained his position as a good student. It gave him hope that he, too, could do it.

'And my parental unit fights so much that they put my elder brother and me to shame,' Akshay added.

Neev fell silent. He wished he had confided in them earlier. Perhaps they would have helped him handle the situation better.

'What is this divorce?' Dharamjeet asked.

'My parents have separated, and they don't live together anymore,' Neev explained. 'I stay with my mother.'

There was sorrow in the scholar's eyes. 'Perhaps that is for everyone's good. When two people are making each other sad, they should stay away from each other.'

'Let's go in search of the mahamantri,' Veda said, changing the subject. 'Wherever he is, the gold coins are bound to be there with him.'

The others nodded. Suddenly, they heard footsteps coming down the corridor. With a finger on his lips to silence the group, Neev crept towards the door on all fours. After peeping out, he quickly crawled back.

'It's Chand and Tara,' he whispered to Dharamjeet.

'What do we do now?' the scholar asked, looking scared.

'I think they might be returning to collect the empty vessels,' Neev replied. As they haven't seen me, I'll hide under the bed with my friends. That will not raise any suspicions in their mind regarding our presence.'

Dharamjeet nodded.

The four children quickly crawled under the bed, while Dharamjeet lay down on the mat on the ground, pretending to sleep.

Pushing the door open slowly, the two brothers entered the room. Seeing the scholar asleep, they kneeled to lift the *thalis*.

Dharamjeet sat up. 'You boys are such hard-workers,' he praised them.

The brothers beamed with happiness.

'We like to do our work with dedication and sincerity,' Tara said.

'Has the maharaja left for Samsa?' Dharamjeet asked.

'Long back,' Tara replied.

'Now that rotten mahamantri is acting like he is the new maharaja. He has given the cook instructions to prepare a feast for him and his friends,' Chand grumbled. 'Who eats a feast at this time of the night?'

'Where is the mahamantri now?' Dharamjeet asked.

'In the *raj darbar*, after sending the *raj darbar* guards home,' Tara said disapprovingly. 'He is awaiting the mountain of food we are preparing for him.' Under the bed, Neev and Veda exchanged excited looks while the other two stared at them in confusion.

'Do you want anything to eat?' Tara asked.

Dharamjeet was all ready to refuse when he remembered the four children. *They must be so hungry*, he thought.

'For some strange reason, I'm very hungry,' he said. 'I would like some food.'

'We will get it for you. Give us a few minutes,' Chand said.

The moment the brothers left the room, the children crawled out from under the bed.

'Are you hungry?' Neev asked.

'The food is for all of you,' Dharamjeet smiled. 'I thought you all must be starving.'

Even at a time like this, when he had lost all his gold coins, Dharamjeet is thinking of us. Some people had such a pure heart, Neev thought.

'After eating, we will go to the *raj darbar*. I'm sure the gold coins will be with the mahamantri,' Neev said.

'I think the same,' Rishi agreed.

'But do we have a plan on how to get the coins back from him?' Akshay asked.

'We will wing it,' Veda said. 'I'm eager to see MM.'

'MM?' Rishi looked puzzled.

'MahaMantri,' she explained.

Hearing footsteps, the four children once again hid under the bed.

Chand and Tara had returned, carrying a *thali* filled with food and a tumbler of water.

'*Mahashaya*, please enjoy your meal while we go and serve the mahamantri,' Chand said.

After the brothers left, Dharamjeet requested the children to eat. They sat around the *thali*, enjoying the royal feast. It was the first time Neev was sharing food with his friends. He had never eaten from a common *thali* before. The loner that he was, he always ate alone in the classroom while his classmates spent their lunch break in the playground. But this eating together was fun. Although he ate only a little, more for the sake of giving his friends company than to satisfy his hunger, Neev was enjoying himself.

'Everything is so delicious,' Veda licked her fingers.

'I love the kheer,' Akshay said, smacking his lips.

'The kheer is my favourite, too,' Rishi said.

Dharamjeet watched them with a smile on his face.

They passed the tumbler of water around, each taking a few sips.

'I have a plan,' Veda said, sitting back with a satisfied smile on her face.

'What is this genius plan of yours?' Akshay asked.

'Chand and Tara will be serving the MM a royal feast,' Veda began.

'Don't tell me that you want to eat again,' Rishi frowned.

'No, dumbo,' Veda shook her head. 'I'm surprised how you became one of the class toppers. If the MM is at the feast, I bet the coins will be by his side. The greedy man won't let them out of his sight even for a single moment.'

'Toppers meaning?' Dharamjeet frowned.

'Toppers are people who top their school. They are a *gurukul's* best students,' Veda explained.

Dharamjeet looked excited. 'So, these two,' he pointed to Neev and Rishi, 'are the best students. Yet for me, all four of you look like toppers.'

Akshay and Veda looked pleased. Veda flung her arms around Dharamjeet. 'You are the best. We will get you your gold coins back,' she promised.

'Let's go attend the feast,' Neev stood up.

Luckily, Neev's fabulous memory helped him remember the number of right turns they had taken from the *raj darbar* to reach the guest room. The others followed him obediently as he took them down the serpentine passages until they stood at the entrance of the court. Luckily for them, there were no guards at the entrance of the court as the mahamantri had sent them home, so that he and his friends could get some privacy. Neev's friends were as enchanted as he was when he had first set his eyes on the *raj darbar*.

The mahamantri sat on the king's throne. Beside him was the bag of gold coins. All around him, occupying the smaller seats usually reserved for Maharaja Veersara's important ministers, sat the mahamantri's evil friends.

'Oh no,' Neev said, hiding behind a pillar. The others, too, hid behind the large pillar.

'What happened?' Rishi asked.

'Kalgiya the sorcerer is here,' he answered in hushed tones, pointing to the man in grey clothes. 'He was the first one to see me at Buddha's sermon. He will recognize me now as the boy from the future.'

The group grew worried. The sorcerer's presence had spoiled their plans.

19

MONKEY TROUBLE

'Now what do we do?' Akshay's face looked grim as he stared at the sorcerer.

'Even if we hide you, Kalgiya will recognize us as the children from the future and be after our lives,' Rishi announced.

For the first time, Veda looked terrified as she studied Kalgiya's hairstyle and his commanding presence.

Only Dharamjeet was quiet.

'Unfortunately, none of us have a Plan B,' Neev said.

Both Neev and Dharamjeet looked crestfallen and exchanged worried looks. The mahamantri sat comfortably on the throne with the confidence that it belonged to him. Kalgiya, sitting by his side, was whispering into his ear. His monkey and parrot were on his lap.

'They look quite alike,' Veda was observing the sorcerer with interest.

'Who?' Akshay asked.

'The MM and Kalgiya,' she whispered. 'If not for the weird hair accessories and the beard, I would say they are twins.'

'You are right,' Rishi said excitedly. 'They must be twins.'

'Why are you getting so hyper?' Veda asked. 'How will this information help us get the gold coins?'

'If they are brothers, there definitely is a greater plan afoot,' Rishi said.

'I'll move closer to them to hear what they are saying,' Akshay offered.

Akshay slowly inched forward until he reached the pillar closest to where the group was sitting. Crouching down, he craned his ear to eavesdrop on them.

The mahamantri was talking about Dharamjeet, while Kalgiya was staring at the court, sniffing the air.

'I can sense a strange energy here,' the sorcerer said.

'There was a boy with him,' the mahamantri explained. 'When the scholar first came to the *raj darbar*, none of us could see the boy. Later, when I went to get the gold coins, the young boy in odd clothes tried to stop me.'

'The boy from the future is here?' Kalgiya looked excited. 'Where is he?'

'I've locked both of them in the dungeon,' the mahamantri replied. 'I thought the boy could pose a threat to my plans, so it was better to get him out of the way. You mean to say that boy doesn't belong to our time?'

Kalgiya nodded. 'Can I see him? I couldn't do anything because the boy was standing so close to Buddha. But now that he is here, I would love to harness his power. It will make me more powerful. I realized that the scholar, too, has some *siddhis* which I can use, and his knowledge will be extremely helpful to me.'

'They both aren't going anywhere,' the mahamantri said. 'You can see them later and do what you want with them. First things first. What are you going to do to help me?'

'I plan to slowly poison the maharaja. Once he is taken care of, you can be the next maharaja as there are no heirs to the throne,' Kalgiya said.

The mahamantri smiled. 'I can't wait, brother,' he said.

'I'll stay here in your room and start the process. Your faithful men will help me,' Kalgiya said, pointing to the men sitting around them. 'You can stay in my house till then.'

They all raised their left hands. The black tattoo was visible on each person's left hand.

Akshay returned quietly and narrated everything he had overheard and what he had seen.

Neev and Dharamjeet were alarmed. They had no clue that Kalgiya wanted to use them for his wicked motives.

'They all must be practising dark magic,' Veda said. 'That's why the similar tattoos.'

'Must be Kalgiya's teammates,' Akshay added. 'If we go near, I can bet on our project that they all will be able to see us.'

'Please don't go around betting on our project,' Rishi scowled. 'We don't need any negative energy around it.'

Before anyone could say another word, the parrot started screeching. The bird flew towards the pillar where they were all hiding. They all stared at the bird.

Feeling a tug on his hand, Neev watched as the sorcerer's monkey pulled his school bag. As Neev's grip loosened, the monkey grinned slyly, seized the bag, and darted down the corridor with the entire group in hot pursuit.

Akshay had taken the lead. He was a hair's breadth away from the monkey when it darted into the open courtyard.

'Oh no,' Akshay moaned as a tree loomed large.

The others had reached the courtyard. They watched the simian clamber up a tree, still clutching the school bag. The parrot flew out and perched beside the monkey.

'Now that is a plot twist,' Veda grumbled. 'An unexpected and an irritating one.'

'I'm not to blame,' Neev said. 'I had no idea that the parrot and monkey were hand in glove. One distracted us while the other grabbed my bag.'

'No one is blaming you,' Rishi consoled him. 'We will buy you a new school bag after we return home.'

'But the berries are in Neev's bag!' Veda said, raising her eyebrows.

'Oh no,' Rishi said. Plonking himself on the ground, he groaned. 'This is getting complicated'

'I have a plan,' Akshay said, looking up at the monkey.

'Finally, someone has a plan,' Veda said. 'It better be good, AK.'

'See this fruit on the ground,' he whispered, pointing to the courtyard littered with fruit fallen from the trees.

'Why have you dropped your voice?' Rishi asked.

'So that the monkey and the parrot can't hear our plans,' he glowered at the two watching them from the branch of the tree. 'Let's throw some fruit at the monkey. Knowing monkey behaviour, he will chuck something back at us, and most probably, it will be Neev's school bag. We can then grab it and go inside.'

'Super plan,' Neev grinned.

They all started gathering the fallen fruit. One by one, they threw it at the monkey. The grin vanished from the animal's face and was replaced by a scowl. Screeching in alarm, the bird flew back into the palace, leaving its friend alone on the branch.

'What a rotten friend the parrot turned out to be,' Veda laughed.

Clutching the bag close to its chest, the monkey watched in dismay the fruit that constantly missed him (as was the plan since none of them wanted to hurt the animal).

'This creature is a tough nut to crack,' Neev groaned. 'I'm tired of chucking fruit at it.'

All the while, Akshay was watching the monkey's antics. Suddenly moving sideways, he dived like a bowler. Akshay's judgment was precise, and the bag landed neatly in his outstretched hands.

'Howzzat?' Akshay cheered. Grabbing the bag, he raised his finger.

Dharamjeet watched with a smile on his face as Neev, Veda, and Rishi engulfed Akshay in a group hug. He was growing very fond of them.

'You are the best catcher,' Neev put his arm around Akshay.

'You are my favourite,' Veda smiled.

'And mine, too,' Rishi thumped his back.

A couple of rats scurried past them.

'Hey, these are the same rodents,' Neev shouted. 'See their colourful tails.'

'Meaning?' Veda looked puzzled.

'While I was talking to Buddha, Kalgiya's pets were

fighting with some eagles. The sorcerer turned the birds into rats to save his monkey and parrot.'

'Oh no,' Veda shook her head. 'That Kalgiya should be turned into a rat himself. It will teach him a lesson.'

There was a look of distaste on Dharamjeet's face. Even Rishi and Akshay looked dismayed.

'But what are the rats doing here?'

'They must have come following the sorcerer,' Dharamjeet explained.

As they walked back into the palace, Rishi said, 'I have a suggestion.'

They all turned to him. 'Let's sneak into the kitchen and mix the berries in the food they will serve at the feast. So, when the mahamantri and his cronies eat the fruit, they will shrink!' he said.

'Wonderful idea,' Dharamjeet said. 'But where is the kitchen?'

'Follow me,' Rishi declared to the rest of them.

He turned around, sniffed the air, and started walking. As he caught a whiff of the smells he was searching for, Rishi's excitement doubled. He led them straight down a corridor into a large kitchen bustling with frenzied activity.

'My nose never lets me down,' he grinned.

Veda was watching him with amazement. 'I had no idea you had this talent,' she shook her head.

'Which one of us will bell the cat…I mean, drop the berries into the *thalis*?' Akshay asked.

'Of course, it will be our star catcher,' Rishi grinned. 'You are the quickest.'

Akshay looked pleased to be entrusted with this important task. Neev handed him his school bag containing the berries.

They watched the large *thalis* being filled with all sorts of food. Counting the *thalis*, Akshay plucked the exact number of berries from the cluster. He then handed Neev his bag.

'How will we distract them?' Neev asked.

None of them had thought of that. His friends looked disheartened.

'Our entire plan hinges on that,' Rishi said.

'Let me help you,' Dharamjeet volunteered.

'What will you do?' Akshay asked.

'Watch me,' Dharamjeet moved sideways until he could see the head cook clearly. Pinning his gaze on the man, he muttered a string of words like he was chanting an incantation.

The children stared at him, wondering what the usually quiet scholar was doing.

'Boys, I have made some kheer for you all,' the head cook announced. 'You all have stayed awake to help me prepare the feast. This is my reward for everybody.'

'Job done,' Dharamjeet smiled.

'What was that?' Veda asked.

'I hypnotized the head cook to do what I wanted him to do. This will give us time to add the berries to the food,' the scholar smiled.

'You know how to hypnotize people?' Neev asked.

'It was a part of my *shiksha*; my guru had taught me this art,' he replied. 'I usually avoid practising it as it's going against the laws of nature. But today, it was the need of the hour. I'll do a penance later and apologize for it.'

The four children flung their arms around Dharamjeet. Delighted by their affection, he engulfed them in a hug.

As Chand, Tara, and the other boys went into the corner to enjoy some of the kheer the cook had laid out for them, Akshay dropped a berry in each bowl of fruit.

'Mission accomplished,' he said as he high-fived his friends.

Even Dharamjeet high-fived Akshay, taking everyone by surprise.

Walking back down the corridor, they hid behind the row of pillars lining the corridor and watched the procession of the cook's helpers march to the *raj darbar* with the *thalis* loaded with food.

'Now, it's time to wait and watch,' Rishi said.

They all held their breaths as the *thalis* were laid out before the mahamantri and his friends.

20

BERRIES TO THE RESCUE

A single question raced through all their minds: when would the mahamantri and his group of friends eat the berries? Would they eat the fruit at the same time? That was the key factor on which the success of their plan depended. If they ate the berries at different times, then the ones shrinking would end up warning the others of danger. What if Kalgiya recognized his berries?

They had to take some risks and decided to just wait it out.

The group, chatting loudly, began devouring the feast. Neev and his friends (yes, he considered Dharamjeet as a friend, too) watched eagerly as the mahamantri's friends gorged on the food. Some ate the savouries first, others the vegetables, and a few started with rice. But no one touched the kheer and the fruit.

There was no sign of the monkey and the parrot. That was a huge relief.

The mahamantri's friends were messy eaters. They chewed noisily, spilled some of the food around them, and slurped the liquids. It wasn't a pleasant sight.

'I would hate to eat with them,' Veda grimaced.

Soon, the group reached their meal's end, and most *thalis* looked empty. Only the fruit was left.

'I'm full,' the mahamantri announced and let out a loud burp. It was as though five elephants had belched together.

'So am I,' Kalgiya said. 'There is no room in my stomach for even a tiny pocket of air.'

'Will they all eat their fruit or leave it there?' Akshay asked apprehensively.

'We need to ensure that they all eat the berries at the same time for our plan to be successful. Leave it to me,' Dharamjeet said. Staring at the mahamantri, he started whispering incantations.

'There is always room for berries. Aren't they our favourite fruit, brother?' The mahamantri's eyes gleamed as he stared at Kalgiya. 'Let's all eat them together,' he announced, lifting the fruit between his fingertips.

The mahamantri's guests held the berry in their hands. They all popped it into their mouths at the same time—in one synchronized move.

'Done,' Dharamjeet whispered. His face was pale; he wasn't happy with what he had done.

The children felt sorry for him. Now, he would have to perform one more penance for it.

As the group chewed the berries, Neev and his friends gazed at them unwaveringly. Their eyes were fixed on the bag of gold coins near the mahamantri.

Within a few seconds, they heard hissing sounds as the mahamantri, Kalgiya, and their nasty group started shrinking.

'I'm burning!' Kalgiya screamed.

'So am I!' The mahamantri wailed.

Screeches, moans, and groans filled the air as everyone in the *raj darbar* started diminishing in size.

'Oh no,' Kalgiya moaned. 'After this disaster, my powers will never be the same. I may even lose them!'

Neev and his friends exchanged delighted looks. This was an unexpected bonus.

'Sometimes, this is how things unfold for evil people,' Dharamjeet said. 'I had a feeling this would happen. Kalgiya imbued the berries with his energy, making them negative. But as they were in Buddha's presence, albeit for a short time, the Enlightened One's positivity ensured that they didn't harm us but only helped us when we needed it.'

'By that logic, it shouldn't harm these tattooed people?' Akshay asked.

'Because their intention is pure evil, it overrides everything and negates the goodness it briefly experienced,' Dharamjeet explained. 'Our intentions were good, so we experienced its positive impact. Since their sole motive was to harm others, they didn't.'

'Makes sense,' Neev nodded.

The screams continued for some time.

Finally, there was complete silence.

As Neev ran into the royal court, the others followed him. Lifting the bag of gold coins beside a thumb-sized mahamantri, he handed it to Dharamjeet. The minister watched him helplessly, unable to do anything. Beside Kalgiya was his bag, but now it looked gigantic in contrast to the mini sorcerer.

'Thank you,' Dharamjeet said emotionally. 'The people of my village will be very happy.'

'One, two, three,' Veda counted, lifting each mini-sized member and dropping them into her school bag. 'Total sixteen.'

'Are you planning to take them back with you?' Akshay nearly shouted.

'No, Akshay,' Veda said firmly. 'But I've definite plans for them all,' she muttered.

Neev and Veda exchanged looks. They had identical grins on their faces.

'What are you two planning?' Rishi frowned.

'To the dungeons,' Neev said.

Neev led the way through the corridors to the guest room, his excellent memory guiding him accurately. From there, following Veda's bubble gum and knitting yarn trail they reached the dungeons, huffing and puffing like they had run a marathon.

When they approached the cells, Veda removed the thumb-sized people from her bag. One by one, she placed them on her ruler and dropped them into the dungeon through the iron grilles. None of the captives had the energy to fight back or even protest. In a few minutes, the entire group had landed inside the dark cell.

Neev and his friends watched them. Though they disliked what they were doing, they had no other option if they wanted to protect the people of Dhwani, save the king from the plot his corrupt mahamantri was brewing, and return Dharamjeet his prize.

They all walked back. Each person was silent and mulling over the events that had taken place. Something continued to bother Neev. Something didn't feel right. As they reached the corridor, he turned around and raced back to the dungeons. His friends followed him.

Once they were back in the dungeons, he removed the remaining berries from his school bag. The cluster had broken, there were exactly sixteen left. He flung the handful of berries through the bars.

'It will take them ages to get to it,' Neev said. 'But it is wrong to leave them in such a condition.'

'That was a noble and kind thing you did.' Dharamjeet looked at Neev with respect. 'For one so young, your sense of right and wrong is sharp. Always hold on to that.'

A rat squeaked. They stared at the rodent as it made its way to the berries. It was followed by its companion. Both had the same funny tail.

'Oh no,' Neev groaned. 'These are the same rats. They will chew all the berries.'

'Nothing can be done now,' Dharamjeet said. 'We did our best for mahamantri's friends, but destiny had different plans.'

They watched the mini-people running helter-skelter at the sight of the rats.

'Evil Kalgiya finally met his match,' Akshay said.

As they left the dungeons, Veda started removing the chewing gum and the knitting yarn from the wall. 'Don't want to spoil the beauty of the palace,' she said.

'Wow,' Akshay said. 'You two are giving us serious goals to always do the right thing.'

Luckily, it came out neatly without leaving any traces of its presence.

After clearing up the chewing gum and knitting yarn trail, they reached the guest room again.

'All done,' Veda said, pulling out the last bit of bubble gum.

Dharamjeet patted her head. 'You all are good children,' he said.

They made their way out of the palace with a spring in their steps and a smile on their faces. It was a pleasant day, and the sun was in a gentle mood. A cool breeze swept past them, making the leaves flutter.

They ambled through forests and fields, stopping frequently to eat some fruit they plucked from the trees and drink water directly from the streams.

All too soon, they entered Dharamjeet's village. Clouds had gathered overhead, thunder rumbled through the sky. Rain began to patter down over them. The parched ground soaked the water greedily, leaving no trace of it. Just a gentle softness and moisture clung to the ground.

Dharamjeet's eyes were brimming with tears as they ran the last stretch to enter his hut. Rain continued to batter the ground. As the sun peeped out from behind the lining of the clouds, a beautiful rainbow appeared in the sky.

From the window, Neev saw Inderjeet leading a group of villagers to his friend's hut.

'I have some news for you,' Inderjeet said.

21

BACK TO THE LIBRARY

Dharamjeet looked at his friend, wondering what news he had for him. Turning to the four children, he exchanged puzzled looks.

Neev studied Inderjeet. He appeared to be peaceful. So, whatever news it was, it must be good.

'How was your journey?' Inderjeet asked.

Dharamjeet waved the bag of gold coins. They jingled and jangled, announcing their presence to everyone.

The villagers looked delighted. Finally, they could see an end to their problems. First, the much-needed rains. Now, the money.

He handed the bag to his friend, explaining the entire sequence of events. Everyone listened as he pointed to the children who had come to his rescue. Neev's story was explained in great detail. The villagers turned to him, awe evident in their eyes.

'So, we need to thank the children from the future,' Inderjeet smiled. 'Our village owes a lot to you all. You are welcome to visit us anytime.'

'Thank you, but we need to get back home,' said Neev.

Dharamjeet looked sad. He was reluctant to let the children go back. But they had to return, as they didn't belong to his time. He embraced them. They, too, hugged him back.

'First, let us take you all to meet someone special,' Inderjeet said. 'Someone whose blessed and holy feet brought rain to our parched land.'

Now, it was NARV and Dharamjeet's turn to look puzzled.

'Who?' Dharamjeet's question went unanswered as the villagers started following Inderjeet down a path.

The rain had left its mark everywhere. Birds perched on the trees were celebrating the arrival of the monsoon. The few animals that were left moved around energetically—a new life had been infused into them. The people had lost their listless and tired looks. The houses shed their bleak facades and bustled with activity.

Neev couldn't believe what he was seeing. A crowd had gathered beside a monk who was sitting in the distance under a large tree. He recognized Dharamjeet's wife in the crowd.

Buddha was here.

Neev's heart raced. He ran the last hundred metres.

'So, we meet again, Neev,' Buddha smiled.

'Dharamjeet received bonus gold coins,' he said excitedly as the words tumbled out of his mouth.

Buddha had a knowing look on his face as he listened to Neev and his friends narrate the adventure with the sorcerer.

'You were right,' Neev said. 'My friends not just came to my rescue, but they also showed me what friendship is all about.'

Buddha nodded. His followers watched Neev curiously. Now they could all see the boy from the future and his friends.

There was a serene expression on Buddha's compassionate face as he looked at Neev and his friends.

'Don't be judgemental and dismiss people before giving them a chance, Neev,' Buddha said.

Neev was silent. He turned around to look at his friends. Then, he stared at Buddha.

'Thank you for trusting me with the responsibility,' he said. 'It brought my friends to me and made me realize the true meaning of friendship. It also gave me a new friend though I won't be able to keep in touch with him.'

Neev flung his arms around Dharamjeet once again. Following him, the rest of his teammates did the same. Their embrace made Dharamjeet emotional; he had grown so attached to them. The children were reluctant to leave Dharamjeet, but they had to go back to their time.

Waving a tearful bye to the villagers, they moved closer to Buddha.

'Always help each other like you did this time,' he said.

Buddha touched their heads one by one. A gentle wind rustled through the trees. Leaves fluttered down, getting entangled in NARV's heads.

As they watched, Buddha faded away before their eyes. Dharamjeet and the villagers disappeared.

NARV was startled to see that they were back in their school library, surrounded by their books. The ceiling fan whirred noiselessly. All around them, their classmates scribbled furiously, trying to complete as much research as they could before the school bell rang.

Neev looked at his friends. They all had amused expressions on their faces.

Biting his lip, Neev pondered over the situation. Was it all a dream? 'Did we imagine that?' he asked his friends.

'No,' Veda replied. 'All of us can't imagine the same thing.'

'I can still feel the caress of Buddha's touch,' Rishi sighed.

'It was a strange and comforting touch,' Akshay said.

As they lowered their heads to complete their project, leaves fluttered down from their heads onto the library table.

22

B.O.A.T.

Several weeks later, NARV submitted their project on the Buddha, hoping for the best. The friendship that had started because of the project continued even after the assignment was completed. The only difference was that now Sunny, Minku, and Siya also joined them during lunch break and free periods. Neev's circle of friends had grown larger. NARV also started hanging around together after school at Neev's house.

The month-long wait for the results wasn't easy on any of them. Sanika Ma'am was as quiet as a statue whenever she entered their class. She gave no hint whatsoever regarding which project had been sent for the inter-school competition. It was supposed to be a surprise.

Finally, the day of the results arrived. The students sat upright in their chairs as Sanika Ma'am and a tall, friendly-looking man in a black suit entered the class.

NARV exchanged puzzled looks.

'Who is the man?' Veda leaned forward and whispered in Neev's ears.

'No idea,' he said.

'Good afternoon, students,' the teacher said. 'I want to introduce you all to Mr Rahil Dubey. He is a member of the Bhopal School Association Board.'

Mr Dubey cleared his throat. 'This year, we changed the competition's previous rules of accepting only one entry from each school. We were happy to receive many excellent assignments, and Shiksha Academy sent us three entries.'

The students exchanged excited looks.

'The three entries were that of Mihir's Mates, Sunny Side Up, and NARV.'

Neev gripped the edge of his desk. From the corner of his eyes, he saw Rishi stiffen. Behind him, Veda sighed heavily. Akshay leaned forward expectantly.

'But the best one was...NARV!'

His last few words were buried under the thunderous applause from the class. NARV's members had already jumped out of their seats and were hugging each other.

'Yay!' Akshay exclaimed.

'We are B.O.A.T.,' Veda grinned.

Neev and Rishi were grinning from ear to ear.

Mr Dubey held a cheque in his hand.

'We will accept it together,' Neev said to his teammates.

NARV walked towards their prize, holding hands.

WINNER
-NARV-

EPILOGUE

BUDDHA ON NEEV

Neev is so confused. I hope his time travel has cleared some of the clutter in his mind. He is struggling to come to terms with his parents' divorce. With his present attitude, he doesn't enjoy the time he spends with either of his parents. But I'm sure that Neev will slowly come to terms with their separation and stop analysing the situation or constantly being upset about it.

Neev must also learn to let go of his suspicious nature and accept gestures of friendship without trying to find hidden agendas. Especially when there are none. At a young age, children make friends easily and fast. But Neev is constantly doubting his classmates' sincerity. He needs a good friend in life, maybe more than just one.

I'm sure that he has learnt that time is both a dear friend and a wicked enemy. Neev will learn to utilize his time well without worrying about the future or crying over the past. He will ensure that he enjoys every single moment of the present which belongs to him and is in his hands.

I entrusted him with the task of escorting Dharamjeet back to his village only to make sure Neev learns to trust his friends and understand the value of friendship and teamwork. I'm proud that he ended up doing both.

NEEV ON BUDDHA

The Buddha lived up to everything I had heard about him. Gentle and peaceful, he remained unaffected by all that was happening around him. The simplicity of his teachings and the ease with which he imparted the eternal truths took me by surprise.

Buddha's message and teachings are philosophies on how to live a good life rather than the principles of religion. I liked Buddha's middle path or the path of moderation. It's all about balance in life.

I'm glad that Buddha gave me a task. I'm also glad that I was thrown into the dungeon. Though I was scared, it brought my friends to me. Without their help, I wouldn't have been able to escape or retrieve the gold coins. I've realized that friends are very important in life. To be honest, it was teamwork that made NARV win the big prize. Sometimes, I have to pinch myself because I can't believe that Rishi and I have become so close. Even Veda and Akshay are quite close to me. In fact, I really miss them on the weekends when we don't meet.

Buddha is right—it's in my hands to make my present life beautiful. So, when I asked Mom to join me in football, she was both surprised and delighted. She agreed instantly.

I just hope she plays well and helps my team win. We need to keep our winning streak going. Last week, I spent two days with my dad. I had so much fun. It was like old times.

Rishi, Akshay, and Veda will be close to my heart. With Sunny, Minku, and Siya joining us, I have a larger circle of friends. Even Sanika Ma'am was shocked to see me doing homework with them. Mom, of course, is delighted that I've made many friends.

I'm looking forward to watching a movie this evening with my new friends.

GLOSSARY

Angavastram: a rectangular shoulder cloth worn by men; it can be plain or with decorated borders and is usually worn with a dhoti and a kurta

Bhool bhulaiya: a maze or a labyrinth

Diya: a small oil lamp made from clay

Gurukul: a guru's home, which serves as a type of school where students live and learn under the guidance of their guru

Katoris: small bowls

Kshama: forgiveness or asking for forgiveness

Mahamantri: senior minister

Mahashaya: sir

Pranam: a respectful greeting

Raj Darbar: royal court

Shiksha: knowledge, learning, and study of a skill, lesson, or instruction

Siddhis: magical powers

Thali: a round plate

ACKNOWLEDGEMENTS

My dad, Motilal Chhabria, is my forever inspiration. Guiding me with his gentle wisdom, both when he was with me in this world and now from beyond the clouds. Dad, you continue to inspire me. My mom, Sheela Chhabria, whose love for reading matches mine. She takes on the twin roles of my biggest critique and cheerleader. Mom urges me to reach out for the stars. My Guru Amma, Sadguru Mata Amritanandamayi Devi; her blessings are my strength. Amma is the wind beneath my wings. Lord Ganesha, for urging me on and lighting my path.

This book owes a lot to two wonderful people: Prerna Mathur, managing editor at Scholastic India, and Ashley Kumar, editor at Scholastic India. Both Prerna and Ashley sent me a flurry of emails urging me to write this story. It was at their insistence that I turned the small chapter book into a middle-grade novel. Their constant reminders pushed the storyteller in me to complete the book. Their enthusiasm was unmatched. Thank you, girls.

ABOUT THE AUTHOR

Rachna Chhabria is a versatile writer who has worked as a creative writing teacher, blogger, columnist and freelance writer for various English newspapers. She enjoys writing quirky characters who take her on crazy adventures. Animal stories are her favourite. Humour and creative nonfiction are her forte. Some of her notable works include *Ganesha's Gifts; Shiva and Parvati in Magadhpur*; *The Giggling Girl; 50 GREAT INDIANS: Extraordinary Lives, Inspiring Tales; Chaos in the Jungle and Other Stories, Festival Stories Through The Year* and *Lazy Worm Goes On A Journey.*

MORE BY THE AUTHOR